S0-AIW-484

THE SUN ALSO RISES

A NOVEL OF THE TWENTIES

TWAYNE'S MASTERWORK STUDIES

Robert Lecker, General Editor

The Bible: A Literary Study by John H. Gottcent

The Birth of Tragedy: A Commentary by David Lenson

The Canterbury Tales: A Literary Pilgrimage by David Williams

Great Expectations: A Novel of Friendship by Bert G. Hornback

Heart of Darkness: Search for the Unconscious by Gary Adelman

The Interpretation of Dreams: Freud's Theories Revisited by Laurence M. Porter

Invisible Man: Race and Identity by Kerry McSweeney

Jane Eyre: Portrait of a Life by Maggie Berg

Middlemarch: A Novel of Reform by Bert G. Hornback

Moby-Dick: Ishmael's Mighty Book by Kerry McSweeney

Paradise Lost: Ideal and Tragic Epic by Francis C. Blessington

The Red Badge of Courage: Redefining the Hero by Donald B. Gibson

The Scarlet Letter: A Reading by Nina Baym

Sons and Lovers: A Novel of Division and Desire by Ross C Murfin

To the Lighthouse: The Marriage of Life and Art by Alice van Buren Kelley

The Waste Land: A Poem of Memory and Desire by Nancy K. Gish

THE SUN ALSO RISES

A NOVEL OF THE TWENTIES

Michael S. Reynolds

TWAYNE PUBLISHERS • BOSTON
A Division of G. K. Hall & Co.

The Sun Also Rises: A Novel of the Twenties
Michael S. Reynolds

Twayne's Masterwork Studies No. 16

Published by Twayne Publishers
A division of G. K. Hall & Co.
70 Lincoln Street, Boston, Massachusetts 02111

Copyediting supervised by Barbara Sutton
Book Production by Janet Zietowski
Typeset in 11/14 Sabon by
Compset, Inc. of Beverly, Massachusetts

Printed on permanent/durable acid-free paper
and bound in the United States of America

Library of Congress Cataloging-in-Publication Data

Reynolds, Michael S., 1937–
The sun also rises, a novel of the twenties.

(Twayne's masterwork studies ; no. 16)
Bibliography: p.
Includes index.
1. Hemingway, Ernest, 1899–1961. Sun also rises.
I. Title. II. Series.
PS3515.E37S926 1988 813′.52 88-1309
ISBN 0-8057-7962-0 (alk. paper)
ISBN 0-8057-8015-7 (pbk. : alk. paper)

Contents

Note on References and Acknowledgments

The text to which I refer in this book is the Scribner Library paperback edition issued by Charles Scribner's Sons (1926, 1952). All references are parenthetical. After twenty-five years of teaching *The Sun Also Rises,* I cannot possibly recall all of the sources of my marginal and typed notes. Most obviously I have been influenced by the work of Carlos Baker, Earl Rovit, Bob Stephens, and Phil Young. These and other scholars have become part of the permanent critical landscape, which has, of course, played a role in my own reading of the novel.

The manuscripts to which I refer are housed in the Hemingway Collection at the John F. Kennedy Library in Boston. The manuscript quotations have all appeared previously in print in either my "False Dawn" essay or in Frederic J. Svoboda's book, *Hemingway and "The Sun Also Rises."* Some of the historical background for the text is derived from my essay—"The Sun in its Time: Recovering the Historical Context"—*New Essays on The Sun Also Rises* (1987) that Linda Wagner has edited for Cambridge University Press.

Ernest Hemingway, ca. 1925
From the Papers of Patrick Hemingway.
Courtesy of the Princeton University Library.

Chronology: Ernest Hemingway's Life and Works

1899 21 July. Ernest Miller Hemingway born in Oak Park, Illinois. Father is a strongly religious doctor and naturalist; mother, a concert-quality contralto and voice teacher. Attends Oak Park public schools and Congregationalist churches; writes for school newspaper and literary magazine. Spends summers in the woods at family summer home at Lake Walloon, Michigan.

1917 Graduates from Oak Park High School; writes for Kansas City *Star* from October until following April.

1918 Rejected by the armed forces because of his genetically weak eye, joins Red Cross ambulance unit in Italy. Wounded by shrapnel and machine gun fire 8 July. Spends rest of year at Red Cross Hospital, Milan, Italy, and falls in love with his nurse, Agnes Von Kurowsky.

1919 Returns to Oak Park. Starts writing short stories. Agnes rejects him. Summers at the lake; spends autumn writing.

1920 Takes job in Toronto and writes free-lance for the Toronto *Star.* Returns to Lake Walloon for summer; his mother throws him out for insolence and idleness. In October moves to Chicago. Meets Carl Sandburg and Sherwood Anderson. Also meets Hadley Richardson, of St. Louis. In December finds job writing and editing the magazine *Cooperative Commonwealth,* which he holds until its demise in October 1921.

1921 3 September marries Hadley Richardson. Takes part-time job with Toronto *Star* to write feature stories in Europe. In December, he and Hadley sail for Paris.

1922 In Paris meets Ezra Pound, Gertrude Stein, James Joyce, and William Bird, newsman and publisher. Pound asks him to contribute to Bird's Three Mountain Press modernist experiment in prose. As roving correspondent for Toronto *Star,* covers the

	Genoa Conference on International Economics, the Greco-Turkish War, and the Lausanne Peace Conference. In December Hadley loses suitcase containing all his literary manuscripts.
1923	Vacations with Hadley in Switzerland and visits Ezra Pound in Rapallo, Italy. Makes first trip to Spain; in July returns to Pamplona with Hadley for his first San Fermin festival. Covers Ruhr troubles for Toronto *Star.* Contributes "My Old Man" to *Best Short Stories of 1923*. Robert McAlmon's Contact Editions publishes *Three Stories and Ten Poems.* Returns with Hadley to Toronto in August for birth of first child. Resigns from *Star* to return to Paris.
1924	In Paris becomes associate editor for Ford Maddox Ford's *transatlantic review.* Three Mountain Press edition of *in our time* published in Paris.
1925	Hemingways meet F. Scott Fitzgerald, Archibald MacLeish, Sara and Gerald Murphy, Pauline Pfeiffer, Kitty Cannell, Harold Loeb, and Pat Guthrie and Duff Twysden. Publishes in *This Quarter*; Boni and Liveright publish *In Our Time.* Pamplona festival with Hadley, Bill Smith, Loeb, Guthrie, and Twysden gives him basis for beginning *The Sun Also Rises.* Finishes manuscript in the fall. Writes *Torrents of Spring,* a satire on Sherwood Anderson. Hemingways spend Christmas in Schruns, Austria.
1926	Liveright turns down *Torrents,* enabling Hemingway to break contract and sign new contract with Scribners, establishing a life-long partnership. *Torrents* published. Hadley begins a separation from Ernest in August; in November, authorizes him to start divorce to marry Pauline Pfeiffer. *The Sun Also Rises* published in October.
1927	10 May, marries Pauline Pfeiffer in Paris. *Men Without Women* (short stories) published.
1928	Begins writing *A Farewell to Arms* and leaves Paris for Key West, Florida. Second son born by caesarean section in Kansas City, Missouri. 6 December, Clarence E. Hemingway, Ernest's father, commits suicide.
1929	Returns with Pauline to Paris. *A Farewell to Arms* published.
1930	Returns to Key West with Pauline; visits Wyoming, where he breaks his arm in a car accident.
1931	Third son born in November by caesarean section; Pauline advised not to become pregnant again.
1932	Publishes *Death in the Afternoon.*

1933 First visit to Cuba. Publishes *Winner Take Nothing* (short stories); visits Paris on way to safari in British East Africa.

1934 Returns from safari; purchases fishing boat *Pilar.* Starts book on Africa.

1935 Publishes *Green Hills of Africa.*

1936 Publishes "The Short Happy Life of Francis Macomber" and "The Snows of Kilimanjaro." Meets Martha Gelhorn; becomes instantly infatuated. Spanish Civil War begins; contributes money to provide two ambulances and agrees to cover war for North American Newspaper Alliance.

1937 Late March, goes to Spain. Assists filming Loyalist propaganda film, *The Spanish Earth.* Having affair with Martha Gelhorn. Returns to Spain and Martha in fall. Publishes *To Have and Have Not.*

1938 Returns to Key West in January; back to Spain and Martha in March. Publishes *The Fifth Column and the First Forty-Nine Stories.*

1939 Moves to Cuba with Martha Gelhorn. Begins writing novel on Spanish Civil War.

1940 Publishes *For Whom the Bell Tolls.* Divorce final from Pauline. 21 November, marries Martha Gelhorn. Purchases Finca Vigia in Cuba for their home.

1941 Six month trip to China. Pulitzer Prize for Fiction Committee unanimously chooses *For Whom the Bell Tolls*; President of Columbia University vetoes selection; no prize for fiction that year.

1942 Edits *Men at War.* Runs a private intelligence service in Cuba approved by the U.S. Embassy.

1944 In May, both he and Martha return to Europe as war correspondents. Late May, meets and becomes infatuated with Mary Welsh. Suffers severe concussion in London car crash. July–January 1945, is war correspondent attached to the U.S. Fourth Infantry.

1945 Returns to Cuba. Mary Welsh moves into Finca Vigia; obtains divorce from her husband. Martha Gelhorn's divorce from Hemingway final 21 December.

1946 14 March, marries Mary Welsh, fourth and final wife. Remains in Cuba.

1947 Writing *The Garden of Eden.*

1948 Takes Mary back to his favorite places in Italy. Becomes enamored with young Adriana Ivanich, 19.

1949	Returns to Cuba in spring; works on *Across the River and into the Trees.*
1950	Spends first three months primarily in Venice. Returns to Cuba. Publishes *Across the River and into the Trees.* Writes first draft of *Islands in the Stream.*
1951	Starts and finishes *The Old Man and the Sea.* Deaths of mother, Grace Hall Hemingway, in June, and of Pauline Pfeiffer in October.
1952	Publishes *The Old Man and the Sea.*
1953	Wins Pulitzer Prize for Fiction. Spends summer in Spain, following the bullfights. In August, goes to Kenya for second safari.
1954	Safari ends with two plane crashes in twenty-four hours; reported dead. Suffers severe concussion and serious burns. Returns to Venice in March and to Cuba in July. In October, receives Nobel Prize for Literature.
1955	Starts new African book; participates in filming of *The Old Man and the Sea.*
1956	Spends fall in Spain, following bullfights, and November–January in Paris.
1957	Returns to Cuba depressed. Helps in effort to have Ezra Pound released from St. Elizabeth's and treason charges dropped. Starts *A Moveable Feast.*
1958	Rents house in Ketchum, Idaho. While there, Batista falls, and Castro takes over Cuban government.
1959	Buys home in Ketchum. From May through October follows the Antonio Ordonez and Dominguin bullfights in Spain. Late fall, returns to U.S., hunts and rests in Idaho.
1960	After seven months in Cuba, returns to Spain where he suffers serious bouts of paranoia and depression. In November, enters Mayo Clinic for electroshock treatments. *Life* magazine publishes part of bullfight story as "The Dangerous Summer."
1961	By April, depression is suicidal; hospitalized twice in Ketchum; readmitted to Mayo Clinic 25 April. Returns to Ketchum 30 June. Commits suicide with shotgun morning of 2 July.

1 Historical Context

When Hemingway arrived in Paris at Christmas, 1921, he was not prepared for the culture shock of the marginal artists, idle rich, serious painters and writers, youthful rioters, jazz musicians, black dancers, and touring Rotarians who made up a permanent but continuously shifting American/British colony in the City of Lights. This was the generation that Gertrude Stein helped label "lost," the generation of the Jazz Age. It was never really lost, nor was it at all times jazzy. It was the generation that drank more than it should have because it was illegal to drink in the United States during Prohibition; the Volstead Act (1919–33) had made half the country into criminals. In Paris, Americans were conspicuous consumers of alcohol in clubs, bars, and cafés that catered to them almost exclusively. Most Americans spoke little or no French; there was no need, for they seldom engaged natives in any real conversation. Except to provide services, few native French or Spanish appear in *The Sun Also Rises*.

This was the postwar generation, and many of Hemingway's Paris contemporaries were combat veterans. He himself bore his accidental wounding in Italy with stoic bravery, letting people think he had behaved more heroically than he had. War experience was the entry fee, the badge that got one into the select club of insiders. But the war was not over. In Germany, inflation caused by the war debt turned the country into a tourist's dream and a native's nightmare. Berlin became the most decadent town on the continent; the next war—and everyone knew there would be a next war—had to result from the Paris peace settlement that had cut the heart out of Germany's industrial economy. In the Balkans, Turks were fighting Greeks. In Italy the Fascists swept Mussolini into power, and the future was made visible. In Paris, the jazz played late in the clubs and the cheap champagne flowed on. What was the point of worrying about the next war? No one had faith any longer in the politicians who had started the last war. No one believed any longer in the values that had taken the men into the trenches of the Great War, as it was now called. Honor, glory, country no longer moved this generation of which Hemingway was a part.

Politics did not interest this generation. At home the country elected Warren G. Harding, who headed the most corrupt administration since Grant's. His secretary of the interior sold the U. S. Navy's oil reserves at Tea Pot Dome to the Sinclair Oil Company. No matter. The country continued to elect conservative Republicans until the bottom fell out of the stock market and the Jazz Age went bust. The conservative politics of the twenties in America were reflected in the rise of reactionary hate groups like the Ku Klux Klan, the popularity of fundamentalist ministers, the falling numbers of union membership, the increased efforts to purify the country by censoring books and movies, and a general anti-intellectual attitude. Many of the Paris expatriates had left their native soil to avoid dealing with this conservative tide.

Those were the days of the silent movies; those were the days when Chaplin was king. And they all came to Paris: the movies played along the grand boulevards and their stars played in the Paris clubs, drinking and dancing themselves silly. Or else they came to Paris for a quick divorce and a new wardrobe. Or they came to Paris like Jack Dempsey to cash in on his name and make a movie called *So This Is Paris*. Dempsey, Babe Ruth, Red Grange (football), Bill Tilden (tennis), Bobby Jones (golf) and other sports figures were the other heroes of the Jazz Age. Their faces were better known than those of most political figures, and they were immortalized in newsreel footage, the first generation of highly paid superstars.

Those were also the days when women changed the rules of the mating game. From decorously trailing the floor, their skirts rose almost overnight to above their knees. Whale-bone corsets disappeared along with the pinched waist and the opulent bosom. Flat was faddish; breasts were bound and dresses were as whispy as possible. The lovely, long tresses of the previous age disappeared as hair was bobbed. The lipstick-stained cigarette was a sign of the times, and the really daring young women smoked in public. The waltz that had shocked an earlier generation was now too sedate; ministers and keepers of the public morals were enraged by the Charleston, the Black Bottom, and other jazzy dances. This was the first generation of American women to drink and smoke, the first generation to vote (1919), and the first generation for whom divorce was a reasonable solution to a bad marriage. Those who could afford a trip to Paris took advantage of easygoing divorce laws that allowed much quicker divorces than those at home.

Everything was happening so quickly; speed was synonymous with the times. The automobile, no longer funereal black, increased in horsepower, beauty, and cost. Installment buying arrived just in time to allow most middle-class families to purchase the latest version of the American Dream. But the automobile was only the most obvious piece of consumer technology. Elsewhere, the airplane was speeding up mail delivery and by 1927 would fly the Atlantic with the Jazz Age's darling, Charles Lindbergh, at the controls. Soon the Lindy Hop was another record playing on the phonographs that carried the Jazz Age music into the American living room. Black jazz musicians and singers were now being heard in rooms where no Black American could enter. The Blues caught the American ear in Chicago and in Paris. Bessie Smith moaned her "Cemetery Blues" while Ruth Etting was "Shaking the Blues Away" and Ethel Waters told them 'bout "Oh Daddy." This was the generation that learned how to kiss from the movies and how to dance from records. In 1925 Black dancers and musicians took Paris by storm. Revue Negre was the rage, and its chief attraction, Josephine Baker, was the toast of the town.

Hemingway's Paris was also the intellectual center of the 1920s in literature, painting, dance, and music. In Paris, Diaghilev's Ballet Russe employed modernist painters to do sets and costumes for his innovative choreography to contemporary music. In Paris, Gertrude Stein had been conducting her experiments in prose since just after the turn of the century. In her salon one could see her remarkable collection of modernist painting, perhaps even meet Picasso, Braque, Gris, or Miró. Sylvia Beach's bookstore, Shakespeare and Company, was a writer's haven and post office. Soon after Hemingway arrived, Beach published the novel that no one else dared publish—James Joyce's *Ulysses*. At the same time, Ezra Pound, mid-wife to a generation of young writers, was editing T. S. Eliot's *The Waste Land*. Eventually all the writers of the age passed through Paris, and many of the young ones became Hemingway's acquaintances: Archibald MacLeish, John Dos Passos, Sinclair Lewis, e. e. cummings, Louis Bromfield, Donald Ogden Stewart, Dorothy Parker, and F. Scott Fitzgerald, to name a few. Nowhere else could a young writer so quickly make contact with the leading edge of his times than in Paris. In less than a year Hemingway plugged into a cultural network that made him well-known before he published a single word. That was what Paris could do for a man in those days.

2 The Importance of the Work

Twentieth-century American writers were a little slow to emerge, and by 1920 America still had not produced a modernist novel. In England before and during the Great War, such novelists as Joseph Conrad, Ford Madox Ford, D. H. Lawrence, and Virginia Woolf were laying down the parameters of modernism. By the end of the Great War in France, André Gide had already published *The Immoralist, Strait Is the Gate,* and *The Caves of the Vatican*; Marcel Proust began publishing the several volumes of his *Remembrance of Things Past* in 1913. James Joyce's *Dubliners* and *Portrait of the Artist as a Young Man* both appeared before 1920. In America, however, not a single novel that we now think of as a modernist work had yet been written. Ezra Pound, the permanent expatriate, spent the early part of the century in England fomenting Imagism, which did affect American poets, and Gertrude Stein, the other famous expatriate, was in France writing her experiments for a limited audience. But the closest America had to a modernist in fiction was Sherwood Anderson.

Somehow it took the Great European War to set the American writer free. Until 1920 the fictional scene continued to be dominated by the old guard: William Dean Howells, Mark Twain, and Henry James. By 1920, Twain and James were dead and Howells was moribund, but that triumvirate's influence held sway nonetheless. Two decades into the century, the "young" American writers who promised to be the future of the novel were Joseph Hergisheimer, Theodore Dreiser, Ellen Glasgow, and Edith Wharton—each a follower of dated fiction ideas. Thus when Sinclair Lewis, Scott Fitzgerald, John Dos Passos, and Ernest Hemingway appeared between 1920—26, they had the field to themselves. They defined what a modern American novel should look like, how it should be structured, and what its subject matter might be.

In 1926, *The Sun Also Rises,* as a survey of its critical reception shows, was as disturbing as anything new can be disturbing. The book-reading public was not prepared for its ironic understatement, its cryptic dialogue, or its hard-drinking and openly sexual characters. These were not the mindless flappers of popular fiction, and the book had nothing to do with the movies, popular music, or discreet visits to speak-easies. This was the real thing. The characters were truly the war-wounded, the spiritual bankrupts of the postwar period. There was nothing quite like it in print, nothing quite as intense. It was not a book that one could keep at a distance: one either participated in the narrative or one did not understand it. The author did not tell his readers how to react or how to judge the action; they had to become involved. By 1926, no young writer was trying to imitate Howells, Twain, or James. The modernist novel had finally arrived in America, and our fiction was never to be the same thereafter.

One reason that we continue to read *The Sun Also Rises* is for its historical importance: it was one of the early and permanent building blocks for the fiction of our century. Writers who followed Hemingway could not ignore his novel. Its dialogue became faddish, invading the world of the hard-boiled detective, and it remains current to this day. The novel also contributed to the demise of the intrusive author telling his readers how to react or leading them by the hand. Jake Barnes became a prototype for the antihero, the modernist man whose greatest virtue is that he manages to survive. Jake's relatives abound in our time. Brett Ashley's sophisticated sexual attitudes, casual use of money, and mod dress went on to influence fictional women and movie fantasies. Hemingway's use of sexual material signaled the end of the "little bell" that Howells once spoke of hearing in the back of his editorial mind, the bell that told him when a writer had overstepped the bounds of decorum. Like most important writers, Hemingway pushed up and outward those invisible boundaries of taste; his fight for sexual terrain in 1926 made it that much easier for the American writers who came after him.

The audience for whom *The Sun Also Rises* was written is now long in the tooth or in the grave. Yet what happened that summer in Pamplona continues to interest us. Like all good novels, it is both time-bound and timeless. Firmly anchored in the mid-1920s, it asks those timeless questions that Auden told us were easy to ask but whose answers were difficult to remember: How shall we be? Who and how shall we love? In what shall we believe? *The Sun Also Rises* is, therefore, more than a historical artifact, more than a moral barometer of its own time. Reading the novel today tells us a good deal about our values. The way we react to Jake Barnes's dilemma tells us something about ourselves. If Hemingway's characters find themselves in a world not of their own making, if they must lead their lives amid the broken promises of their political leaders, if they cannot find a system of belief that sustains them, if they seem to drift aimlessly having no moral compass for direction, it is because they are a bit like us. They are citizens of the twentieth century, citizens who did not want war, did not choose the economic forces that rule their lives, did not choose their psychological problems. Neither did we. When we compare our lives with these fictional ones, we have a device for measuring our own condition. If we do not approve of Brett's behavior, that tells us something about our own moral position. If we sympathize with Jake's difficult decisions, we have learned something about ourselves.

3 Critical Reception

Today *The Sun Also Rises* is established as a classic fiction read and studied in almost every American college and university. It has been translated around the world. In Japan and Russia, at this very moment, students are reading this text, a little confused about Jake and Brett but eager to be in Paris nonetheless. When historians and social scientists write about the twenties, they quote from Hemingway's novel as if it depicted real lives. Such widespread and positive reception was not always the case.

In 1926, reviewers of Hemingway's first serious novel fell into three camps: the repulsed, the antiexpatriate, and the effusive. Like Hemingway's mother, the repulsed reviewers were morally offended by the life-style depicted in the novel. The continuous drinking, occasional fornication, profane language, lack of religious belief, and pervasive lack of sustaining values, many found offensive. The book had no admirable hero, nor did it punish vice. The older reading generation in 1926 still expected a woman like Brett Ashley to be suitably punished for her promiscuity by novel's end. In Cincinnati, it was seen as a book that began nowhere and ended in nothing, a study in futility, a most unpleasant book. A Chicago reviewer was angry at the talent Hemingway appeared to be wasting on trivial characters and drunken conversation. In Springfield, Illinois, the reviewer resented the lack of plot and character development. This kind of reaction was probably closer to the average response than were the more literate reviews, for Jake Barnes and his set of "nice friends" were calculated to offend the morally rigid middle class. The *Sun Also Rises* is still capable of stimulating such response. Wherever book-banners gather today in the name of public morality, they are sure to mention it.

A more interesting negative response came from East Coast reviewers who had a program for American fiction that Hemingway's novel, for one reason or another, did not fit. Some simply objected to what they took to be the glorification of the expatriate life. (How they could read the novel and think that expatriatism was being glorified says a lot about Hemingway's ability to describe his setting; see chapter 6 for more on this topic.) The American expatriate in Paris had become, by 1926, something of a media cliché as well as a topic for debate. At Burguete, Bill Gorton twits Jake about his expatriate life in which he never works and lives off the generosity of women. Not working, I suspect, was the burr under the reviewers' saddles: in America, real men worked hard and steadily; they did not sit about Paris sidewalk cafés drinking and talking.

There was, in 1926, a wider and more intellectual debate about the program American fiction should be following. One school of criticism held that American writers should remain at home on native soil writing about typically American experiences and striving to write the Great American Novel. No one was quite sure that the Great American Novel was, but many felt they would know it when they saw it. Sinclair Lewis and Sherwood Anderson fit this program, as did Willa Cather and Ellen Glasgow. William Carlos Williams epitomized the native soil school of poetry, as opposed to the Ezra Pound international school. *The Sun Also Rises,* no matter what its merits, was certain to offend the "America first" readers. Allen Tate, one of the Agrarians who advocated native soil fiction, found little to admire in *The Sun Also Rises.* He found the characters offensive and undeveloped, the narrator sentimental beneath his "hard-boiled" facade. *Dial* magazine, whose darling was Sherwood Anderson, thought the characters shallow and the action equally without significance. The *Saturday Review of Literature* found it difficult to imagine a more dreary or aimless setting or a more worthless bunch of expatriates, all of whom were recognizable if you frequented the Montparnasse cafés. *Time* magazine found the novel boring, Jake sad, and Brett an imitation from Michael Arlen's *The Green Hat.*

The enthusiastic reviewers did not object to the international aspect of *The Sun.* Many of them had written guarded but positive reviews of Hemingway's first book, *In Our Time* (1925), and were pleased to see their initial judgments confirmed. The *New York Times* admired Hemingway's dialogue, his "gripping" story, and his "lean, hard, athletic narrative prose." Those adjectives describing Hemingway's style have since been permanently printed on the collective mind of America. The athletic metaphor is probably less than accurate, but it sounded fine in 1926, and it is with us still. Conrad Aiken's long review in the *New York Herald* found the novel exciting but indebted to Anderson, Fitzgerald, and Gertrude Stein. Aiken admired Hemingway's understatement and his control. He found none of the sentimentality that Tate complained of. Yes, the characters and their situation were sordid, but Hemingway's dignity, his detachment, and his dramatist's sense of dialogue saved the novel.

No matter which side of the Atlantic they favored, the professional reviewers all recognized Hemingway's considerable talent. They agreed that he had a gift for writing convincing dialogue. Some saw that the effect of the dialogue was to mean almost exactly the opposite of what it seemed to say. In other words, they understood Hemingway's use of ironic understatement. No one admired the life-style of Hemingway's characters, nor did they approve the loss of guiding values. Some saw these characteristics as merely autobiographical failings of the author. Others understood that Hemingway, the author, was not his characters, and that he had done a remarkable job of presenting the "rotten crowd." The prevailing disillusionment of the novel and the sense of futility that haunts the characters were difficult for even the least sophisticated reviewer to miss. But the reviewers were divided on whether Hemingway was to be applauded for depicting these less than savory lives.

As for literary indebtedness, some saw Sherwood Anderson lurking behind Hemingway's style, but this was a knee-jerk response from Hemingway's satire on Anderson—*The Torrents of Spring* (1926)—and his use of the older writer in his earliest stories—*In Our Time* (1925). Others commented on Hemingway's use of Gertrude Stein's rhythms and repetitions, which are, in fact, part of his twenties style. But it took no particular training to make this comment, for Hemingway's brief and literary love affair with Stein, the earth mother of expatriate Americans, was well known and much commented on. His use of Stein's "lost generation" epigraph, of course, called even more attention to the enigmatic lady who wanted to be the female Henry James. At least one reviewer saw that Hemingway had learned something from F. Scott Fitzgerald's *The Great Gatsby* (1924), a true debt that would get more attention a generation later. No one suggested that Hemingway had learned anything from James Joyce, but almost everyone thought that Brett Ashley looked and acted a lot like a similar lady in Michael Arlen's *The Green Hat* (1924). It was said that Lady Duff Twysden had been the model for both fictional women. Today no one remembers *The Green Hat,* nor should they; to read it is to wonder what those early readers saw that seemed so similar.

The initial furor over *The Sun* eventually settled. Hemingway's career continued on schedule: book followed book to increasing sales and recognition. But nothing of critical significance was written about his first novel through the rest of the Jazz Age, the Great Depression, and World War II. By 1951, when *The Sun* was a quarter of a century old, Carlos Baker wrote a retrospective article about how the novel had aged gracefully. The article was the first useful statement about the novel since the early reviews. An entire generation of new readers were coming to Hemingway at about the same time that the American universities were doubling and tripling enrollments with the postwar students. American literature was on its way to becoming a respectable field of study, and novelists like Hemingway began to appear in the college classroom.

In 1952 two major critical books appeared almost simultaneously: Carlos Baker's *Hemingway, The Writer as Artist* and Philip Young's *Ernest Hemingway.* Both academics saw patterns in Hemingway's fiction that remained central to all future discussions of *The Sun Also Rises.* Baker's *Sun* chapter, "The Wastelanders," called attention to Hemingway's mythological methods, which he compared with those of Joyce and Eliot. Here for the first time it was suggested that there was more intellectual content to Hemingway's fiction than appeared on the surface. Baker also gave considerable background on Hemingway's professional career and the literary history of the novel's creation. Young's book called attention to psychological patterns in Hemingway's canon, particularly the repeated use of wounded men whose external wounds run parallel to their internal and psychological problems. Jake Barnes and the other war veterans of the novel fit nicely into Young's perceived patterns. Both Baker and Young called attention to Hemingway's connection with the spirit of Eliot's *The Waste Land,* and both recognized that there was a good deal of conscious artistry in the novel's structure.

Within two years of the Baker and Young books, Hemingway was awarded the Nobel Prize for Literature. When he died by his own hand in 1961, he was a piece of the literary canon, a part of the mainstream. *The Sun Also Rises* and *A Farewell to Arms* became, during the turbulent 1960s, the Hemingway novels of choice, read and studied in high schools and colleges. The second wave of criticism spent unwarranted effort distinguishing between Hemingway's characters and their real-life prototypes. This game lasted until the prototypes all went under the earth; today readers have little interest in whether Duff Twysden really behaved as Brett Ashley did in Pamplona. Another somewhat forced critical approach was the attempt to construct a continuum for the Hemingway hero. The thesis assumed that Hemingway wrote essentially about himself, that his heroes aged as he aged, and therefore, that each central character was an older version of the previous one. This view made sense until we began to examine the characters in whiter light. Now the continuum approach to Hemingway seems to say more about the critics' needs than about Hemingway's art.

The incidence of significant critical articles increased steadily between 1960 and 1987, spurred on by several key books. In one of these Hemingway studies published in 1963 and revised in 1986, Earl Rovit makes further refinements on the teacher-pupil relationships in Hemingway's fiction and Hemingway's "code." Rovit's excellent *The Sun* chapter probably increased its presence in the college classroom. Throughout the second generation of *Sun* criticism, critics have periodically reassessed their inheritance. Revisionist efforts were made to rehabilitate Robert Cohn from goat to a more admirable role; Jake Barnes's narrative voice began to receive attention, as did the novel's skewed timetable. Connections were seen between *The Sun* and other seminal works: *The Waste Land, Don Quixote,* Imagism, Grail legends, and pilgrimages. Since 1976 there have been new textual studies based on the manuscript and efforts made to restore the full language of the first draft.

Since its increased classroom usage, *The Sun Also Rises* has gone through the same changes as the intellectual climate of the country. During the mid-1950s, when the Beat Generation was putting itself on the road, the novel's disjointed and erratic life-style seemed to offer an earlier version of social dissatisfaction. Young, bearded, and sandaled novices went to Paris looking for a fiction long departed. To the activist Vietnam generation, *The Sun*'s missing values and casual sexual relationships were easily assimilated; the book seemed to echo the generation's own dissatisfaction with public values that had produced a debacle. The conservative reaction of the 1970s produced a very different reading, a less sympathetic view of Jake and company's disorder. This latest group to come to the novel does not see anything particularly admirable about the life-style, the drinking, or the casual sex; they find Brett Ashley self-indulgent and irresponsible, and they have little sympathy for Jake Barnes, although he does have a job, which may be the only mark in his favor. Strangely enough, this conservative reading of the novel may be closer to the reaction that Hemingway wanted in 1926. Certainly the political mood of the country is closer to the conservative mood of 1926 than it has ever been since. There is no "correct" reading of *The Sun Also Rises*. Each new generation of readers will bring its own needs to the novel and find there something of its own image. Good books are like that, like mirrors that let us see ourselves. We find in them what we want to find. We should not, therefore, be too harsh on earlier critics whose views now seem dated, for they were once young and certain too.

A READING

Sixty odd years ago, when *The Sun Also Rises* was published, Hemingway's epigraph quoted from Ecclesiastes: "One generation passeth away, and another generation cometh; but the earth abideth forever." The so-called lost generation that spawned the novel is now dead, and no one cares any longer about who were the prototypes for Hemingway's characters, or if he was telling the truth about the far away summer in Pamplona. Other generations have come to the novel, reading it by whatever light was available in their time. Their readings have varied according to bias and taste, time and place, for the novel, like all artifacts made of words, is in a constant state of change. Words may not change shape, but their meanings are as shifty as the sociohistoric context that modifies them.

For present and future readers, the tale of that summer in Paris and Pamplona is an historic document of how we were in those days. Like all historic documents, it requires some explanations, a few footnotes, a bit of focusing, for we are not the audience for whom Hemingway wrote the book. We do not know things that his audience knew. For example, at Burguete when Bill challenges Jake to say something ironic about his request for jam, Jake replies: "I could ask her what kind of a jam they think they've gotten into in the Riff" (114). In 1926, most readers would have known about Spain's involvement in the Riffian war in Morocco; today's reader has never heard of it. Does that really matter? Probably not. Today's reader passes Jake's remark without understanding it but without being disturbed. Over time, more and more of the novel will turn opaque, requiring more explanations. What follows are several perspectives on the novel: analytic, structural, historic, and thematic. Depending upon the reader, some of these commentaries may be unnecessary, others useful. All are meant to be suggestive rather than exhaustive. Certainly they are not absolute, for like all good books, *The Sun Also Rises* is richly various. The reader's response is a function of the knowledge and experience he brings to the novel; *The Sun Also Rises* will not be the same book for him at forty as it was at twenty. It is never the same book twice.

4 The Narrator

A film version of *Hamlet* once began, "This is the story of a man who could not make up his mind." Much the same could be said for Hemingway's narrator, Jake Barnes. One early version of *The Sun Also Rises* manuscript begins: "This is the story about a lady." In another deleted portion of the first draft Jake tells us:

> Now you can see. I looked as though I were trying to get to be the hero of this story. But that is all wrong. Gerald [Robert] Cohn is the hero. When I bring myself in it is only to clear up something. Or maybe Duff [Brett] is the hero or Nino de la Palma [Pedro Romero]. He never really had a chance to be the hero. Or maybe there is not any hero at all. Maybe a story is better off without any hero.
>
> (MS II, 7)

By the time the novel was published, Jake's narrative confusions and hesitant moments had disappeared, but readers continued to have Jake's difficulty with the story: who is the hero and what is the book about?

Perhaps some of Jake's misgivings should have been retained in the published version, for the book has no hero in the time-honored sense of that word. The world of Jake Barnes is without heroes. The heroes did not return from the trenches of World War I. In hundreds of war cemeteries beneath millions of white crosses the heroes of Jake Barnes's generation are neatly buried. Those who remain alive are the walking wounded: Jake with his genital injury, Brett with her lack of self-control, Mike Campbell with his compulsive drinking. In an unpublished preface for the novel, Hemingway wrote:

> There is only this then to say that this generation that is lost has nothing to do with any younger generation about whose outcome much literary speculation occurred in times past. This is not a question of what kind of mothers will flappers make or where is bobbed hair leading us. For whatever is going to happen to this generation of which I am a part has already happened.
>
> There will be more entanglements, there will be more complications, there will be successes and failure. . . . But none of it will particularly matter to this generation because to them the things that are given to people to happen have already happened.
>
> (MS, Foreword)

This generation, coming of age in Eliot's *Waste Land,* temporarily lost hope, abandoned ideals, and discarded dreams. These losses, while not permanent, seemed so at the time. "All the sad young men," as Fitzgerald called them, did not want to think about their immediate past, for it was most unpleasant (World War I). Nor were they particularly fond of their prospective future, for it held no promises other than money, the only value left intact.

Although *The Sun* has no heroes, it has a number of seemingly central characters, who, upon examination, fail the test for centrality. Pedro Romero may look heroic in the bullring, but he does not bear the brunt of the action; he is not changed by the conflict. Nor are Brett Ashley or Robert Cohn changed.

At the end of the novel, Brett is no different than she is when we first meet her. She may think well of herself for not behaving "like a bitch," but we see little prospect that her future will be any different from her past. Cohn, of course, never had a chance to be the central character. The novel's initial view of him is so biased that the reader can never take him seriously. This bias belongs to Jake Barnes—an almost invisible narrator for whom the story has become an obsession. He is the one compelled to tell us about that summer in Pamplona, and he is the one most affected by the action he narrates. If Jake's centrality is not immediately obvious, it is because he only infrequently speaks of his own feelings. However, when we turn the final page, it is Jake's condition we best know: his values, his fears, his failures. He is Hemingway's representative American set down in a foreign country for a test of character which he largely fails. If that description sounds like a Joseph Conrad novel, we should remember that Conrad, who died in 1924, was Hemingway's early modernist model, the first writer to show the novice the way into the heart of the matter.

Throughout the novel Jake unconsciously misleads his reader, for he knows that his is not a pretty story and that he does not behave well during its course. In Paris we are led to believe that the novel's conflict will center on Brett Ashley, for the story seems to be about who will take this beauty to bed. That question becomes obviously anticlimatic: everyone, except Jake, who wants Brett either sleeps with her (Cohn, Campbell, Romero), or could have slept with her (Count Mippipopolous). Exactly why Brett behaves as she does is a matter of debate. Some see her as an insatiable nymphomaniac, but she seems more selective than this label would suggest. Our uncertainty is a result of Jake's own mixed feelings about the lady. In a deleted portion of the manuscript, he says: "As for how Brett Ashley felt and how things that happened to her affected her, I am not a psychologist, I only put down what she did and what she said. You will have to figure that out by yourselves" (MS VI, 56).

The "things that happened to her" were the war, her dead fiancé, and her two disastrous marriages. Hemingway knew his Freudian theory and had also read extensively in Havelock Ellis, an English sexual psychologist whose theories fascinated him.

Although Jake's disclaimer was cut, it remains implicitly there: Jake never does explain why anyone, not even himself, behaves as he does. Hemingway, Jake's creator, provides enough detail to account for the group's amoral and valueless behavior, but he does not explain the detail. That characteristic is one of the differences between the nineteenth-century novel and Hemingway's modernism: the old novel told you how to react to detail; the modern novel typically does not. To read *The Sun Also Rises* perceptively requires us to pay attention to detail and to ask what that detail may indicate about the subtext of the novel and its characters.

Our confusion about the book's theme is due, in part, to Hemingway's own confusion when he began the novel, for it did not start out to be Jake Barnes's story. In fact, in the first forty-page draft, Jake is not even a character in the story, for the novel that Hemingway started to write would have centered on the corruption of the young bullfighter by the Paris crowd at Pamplona. In the first draft we are told: "So I will not judge the gang who were at Pamplona and I will not say that it would be better for Nino de la Palma [later Pedro Romero] to be in his grave than to train with a crowd like that because if he did train with them he would be in his grave soon enough," (MS I, 8). That is the novel Hemingway did not write, although the question of the bullfighter's corruption remains a peripheral issue in *The Sun*. Perhaps Hemingway did not know enough then about the bullfighter to be convincing. Or perhaps he saw that a much better novel could be written about the corruption of Jake Barnes.

At the end of June when Jake Barnes leaves Paris for his annual vacation at the festival of San Fermin, he is content with himself. Through the year he has worked sufficiently hard to save enough money for this event, one of the few pleasures he has. In his rented rooms prior to departure, he carefully balances his bank statement: Jake Barnes is a respectable citizen, a man with a job, which sets him apart from the "rotten crowd" of Left Bank revelers who drink but do not work. A long way from home, Jake Barnes remains an American man: one who works for his living and saves his money. Brett Ashley, Mike Campbell, and Robert Cohn do not work; their money comes from relatives upon whom they are dependent. Being responsible about money is, as we shall see, one of the few values remaining for this generation. So long as money will cover the bills, Jake remains solvent: hotel bills, bar bills, train tickets. But at Pamplona Jake is faced with bills of moral debt that cannot be paid with American dollars or cheap pesetas.

Before examining Jake's disastrous week in Pamplona, we should first examine more closely what we know about this American narrator. We know that Jake was a U. S. Navy pilot flying on the Italian front during the war where he was wounded in the groin. We never see the wound, but we learn implicitly that Jake has all the sexual drives of a normal man but has none of the physical equipment to satisfy those drives. From this information, we must assume that his testicles are intact and his phallus missing. Hospitalized in England, Jake falls in love with his nurse, Brett Ashley: the sexually incapable man and the sexually active woman—a punishment that might have come from Dante's *Inferno*.

We also know that Jake Barnes is a Catholic, which should not be minimized. First of all, being a Catholic in France and Spain—Catholic countries—gives one the advantage of knowing local religious customs. But Jake, by his own admission, is a less than ardent churchgoer. After praying in the Pamplona cathedral for the well-being of people he knows, he prays "that the bullfights would be good, and that it would be a fine fiesta, and that we would get some fishing. . . . I thought I would like to have some money, so I prayed that I would make a lot of money" (97). Jake's voice sounds a lot like Huck Finn who never got what he prayed for because he was praying for the wrong things. Huck was told that he must think of others rather then himself, that he must practice Christian charity. Huck said he saw no advantage to that practice; nevertheless, in the novel he narrates, Huck worries about everyone—friends and enemies.

Jake Barnes is Huck Finn grown up in another century, in a different world. Jake may be, as he professes, a "rotten Catholic," but he does practice Christian charity in his limited way. It is Jake who buys the tickets, makes the plans, and organizes the trip. Like the steer put in with the bulls to quiet them down, Jake shepherds the others about in Pamplona, trying to keep Cohn and Campbell from goring each other. We agree with Cohn: "It's no life being a steer" (141). Like Huck, Jake is the worrier, the one who is left to feel sorry for others when they are in need of it. He even feels sorry for Robert Cohn, whom he has every reason and bias to dislike. At the end, it is Jake who goes to Madrid to help Brett. She may have betrayed him, used him, shamed him, but still he responds to her telegram. His abasement can be blamed on love, but Jake's love can also be seen as the product of specific Christian virtues: long suffering and Christian charity. Unfortunately, he is living in a world that no longer recognizes the validity of those virtues and no longer places special emphasis on religious belief, one of the first major casualties in the Great War. Despite the uneven practice of his faith, Jake remains Catholic enough to believe in the powers of confession. In Pamplona he confesses his sins in a language that Brett does not understand. This novel he narrates is also a kind of confession, but in a language we should understand. Jake Barnes is a man haunted by guilt, and guilt works.

We also know Jake is a Paris journalist who works in an office where acquaintances like Robert Cohn feel free to interrupt him. Jake's job is important to the reader because it is important to Jake: it gives him a sense of identity, a reason to be alive. He is not an expatriate living in a foreign country because he no longer believes in America. Like no others in the novel, Jake works for his money and meets his deadlines. He takes pride in being punctual in a world where none of his friends cares about time. When Brett promises to meet him at the Crillon Hotel at five, she asks him, "I've never let you down, have I?" (29). Jake changes the subject because the answer is, yes, she has, and yes, she will. We should not be surprised that Brett does not make the five o'clock meeting, or that Jake is left there waiting. In this novel of his, Jake does a lot of waiting and is almost always disappointed.

Many men, when faced with disappointment, resort to self-pity to ease their pain. Self-pity, however, is the one emotion that Jake Barnes can ill afford; if he ever starts feeling sorry for himself, he will collapse. He cannot afford to think too much about his sexual condition, for it has no cure but death. One of the few times we see him contemplate his situation, Jake begins by observing himself naked in the mirror, which starts his head working, "the old grievance." One thought leads to another until "I started to think about Brett and all the rest of it went away. I was thinking about Brett and my mind stopped jumping around and started to go in sort of smooth waves. Then all of a sudden I started to cry. Then after a while it was better. . . ." (31). Jake Barnes cannot bear the heavy emotional cost of erotic daydreams. He tells us that he has the rotten habit of imagining the bedroom lives of his friends, but from the context we do not feel that his visions are erotic.

To understand Jake, we must hear his tone of voice. So often in Hemingway, importance resides more in *how* something is said than in the meaning of the words themselves. Granted, we cannot literally hear the voice of Jake Barnes off the printed page, but Hemingway has given us plenty of clues to establish the proper wavelength. When Jake picks up the prostitute, Georgette, he tell us she was pretty until she smiled, exposing a set of bad teeth. When he introduces her at the *bal musette* as his fiancée, he tells us she "smiled that wonderful smile" (18). We know exactly how Jake sounds when he says this. His tone gives exactly the opposite meaning to what the words are saying. When Brett twits Jake about the prostitute he has brought to the *dancing,* she asks him if he has had a lovely evening. Jake replies, "Oh, priceless." Brett laughs. She hears the ironic tone, and from her laughter, the reader also hears. Of course Jake's choice of "priceless" when connected to the whore is also amusing. That's his sense of humor, which is never far removed from his sense of irony. Irony and humor are Jake's main defenses against the sexual affronts and disappointments of his times.

Early in the novel Hemingway provides sufficient clues or indicators to establish Jake's ironic tone. He expects us to remember what we've learned about Jake; the further we read into the novel, the fewer signposts there are to tell us what to hear. At the very end of the novel, Hemingway fully expects us to hear the heavy irony in Jake's voice. When Brett suggests they could have had "such a damn good time together," Jake replies: "Yes. . . . Isn't it pretty to think so." Those readers who view this statement as a happy or at least positive ending to the novel simply have not learned or remembered how ironic Jake is about his own condition.

Besides his ironic sense of humor, another important characteristic about Jake Barnes is that he is no tourist, no casual visitor in another country. Not only does he have a job, but he speaks the language of the country, an ability that immediately gives him an edge. No matter how skilled or educated a man might be, if he cannot speak the language of the country, he is no longer self-reliant but must depend upon others. Jake not only speaks French and Spanish, but he also knows how to get things done in foreign countries. He knows the bars and the bartenders; he knows which wines are good, which restaurants are cheap but good, which trains to take, and where to get off. He shows none of the tourist's anxiety when traveling. He knows how to make hotel reservations, purchase good seats for the bullfights, and find excellent fishing.

Because he speaks Spanish and understands the bullfight, Jake is more than an insider at Pamplona. But understanding the nuances and protocol of the bullring is only part of what Jake brings to Pamplona: he also has *aficion*—the passion for the bullfights. When Jake and his party arrive at Hotel Montoya, Jake tells us that he "had stopped at the hotel for several years," where he could always get a room. Men with *aficion* got special preference from the owner. For those with *aficion,* we are told, Montoya could forgive anything. Jake remarks, "At once he forgave me all my friends. Without his ever saying anything they were simply a little something shameful between us, like the spilling open of the horses in bullfighting." (132). These lines, casually buried in a paragraph, have no markers highlighting them, no special emphasis, but they are absolutely crucial to our reading of the novel.

Jake does not belabor the point, but the reader must realize how important the Pamplona festival is to Jake Barnes. For the several years since the end of the Great War, Jake has made this same pilgrimage to the festival of San Fermin. Year after year he has followed the *riau-riau* dancers down the narrow streets, seen the bulls run past his window, tasted the country wine and simple Basque food, and indulged his passion for the bullfights. From Montoya's point of view, Jake Barnes is a dues-paid club member, "one of us." The week of Pamplona is one of the few pleasures left him. If Jake does not emphasize the point, he has good reason: this summer is the last time he will stay at the Hotel Montoya. He can never return, for he has, in the course of the action, cancelled his membership in the select club of aficionados.

That cancellation, that loss, is really what Jake's novel is about. *The Sun Also Rises* is Jake's confession of guilt, his admission to the corruption of what values he had left to him. At the end of the festival when the hotel bill is ready for payment,

Jake tells us, "Montoya did not come near us. One of the maids brought the bill" (228). Neither Jake's friends nor Jake's behavior are any longer forgivable by Montoya. Montoya's snub is a sign that goes unnoticed by the Paris crowd, but Jake knows exactly what it means. He buries the statement in a paragraph without calling attention to its significance for himself, for he does not want to think about it. What has happened to him at Pamplona is both painful and difficult to discuss. But he gives us the signs, the surface details that have meaning.

• • •

If Jake is less than explicit in his narrative, he should not be considered untrustworthy. He tells us the truth as he sees it, but he never flaunts his shame. No man would. By setting Brett up with Pedro Romero, Jake has placed the young bullfighter at risk. Earlier with Montoya, Jake agreed that Romero had special talent that needed to be protected from women like Brett. Montoya said, "People take a boy like that. They don't know what he's worth. They don't know what he means." Jake agreed, saying "There's one American woman down here now that collects bull-fighters" (172).

This conversation is followed immediately by the scene in which Jake runs into Pedro Romero in the café, and Mike Campbell insults the bullfighter, telling him his bulls have no balls. Jake uses Mike's drunkenness to excuse his rude behavior, but he cannot ignore Brett's request: "You might introduce your friends" (175). The first time Brett saw Romero in the bull ring with his skin-tight green trousers, we were told she could not keep her eyes off of him. Now, in the café swirl of drunken jokes where only Jake and Romero speak Spanish, Brett needs no special language skills to communicate with the young Spaniard. It is at that moment Montoya enters the café. Jake says, "He started to smile at me, then he saw Pedro Romero with a big glass of cognac in his hand, sitting laughing between me and a woman with bare shoulders, at a table full of drunks. He did not even nod" (177).

This is the crucial scene with which Hemingway, when he thought the story would relate the corruption of the bullfighter, began the first draft of the novel. Here, in the final text, this scene has a double focus not present in the first draft. The reader's attention is focused primarily on the Brett-Jake-Romero relationship that will continue to create conflict through the remainder of the novel. But Montoya's brief appearance should remind the reader that Jake is sacrificing much more than his personal dignity by acting as Brett's procurer; he is also giving up his special status in Montoya's club of insiders. If Jake does not call our attention to this point with flashing lights, we must remember that as narrator Jake is telling a story of which he is not particularly proud. It is, as Hemingway once told Scott Fitzgerald, "a hell of a sad story."

5 Structural Unity

Any graph of *The Sun*'s structure will reveal that it is not, in the nineteenth-century sense, a well-made novel with an introduction, conflict, rising action, turning point, falling action, denouement. In its present form, the novel's structure seems curious and arbitrary. The reader of traditional novels expects early in the game to recognize the central character and to understand the conflict that drives the action. At first reading, *The Sun* appears to center on Brett Ashley, and the conflict seems to concern who will take her to bed. As we have already noted, neither assumption is correct. Jake Barnes is the central character and the driving conflict is internal with him. That neither conclusion is obvious until we reach the novel's end is the result of erratic planning on Hemingway's part; it was, after all, his first novel.

The novel he started to write—about the corruption of the bullfighter—would have looked perfectly traditional if he had been able to carry it through. That Ur-novel began in Pamplona on the first day of San Fermin with the hotel owner talking to the narrator about the need for protecting the young bullfighter from predatory women. We then saw that the designing female wanted to seduce the bullfighter and that the narrator was caught between two needs: his desire to be an insider in Pamplona and his need to please the woman. With the conflict clearly established, the narrator tells us: "To understand what happened in Pamplona you must understand the quarter in Paris" (MS I, 10). With that simple trick, Hemingway was going to flash the action back to Paris where the novel we know begins. This structure would have been immediately recognizable as the oldest in the world—in medias res—the structure of epics and a good deal of pulp fiction: get the hook into the reader with a key scene and then flash back to the beginning to write the introduction of place and character. When Hemingway eliminated the opening Pamplona scene, he left us worrying the wrong hook: Cohn and Brett.

As a result of Hemingway's radical surgery on the opening chapters, we do not see clearly the central issue of Jake Barnes's corruption until we are well into the book. Had Hemingway been in complete control of his material in first draft, the result may have been less interesting than the novel we have. The final narrative works because it is loosely planned, which allows for spontaneity. One of the writing tricks that Hemingway studied with Gertrude Stein and seems to have been half following here is the trick of living in the work as it goes along, letting each day make up its own action. Hemingway knew that he was combining the two previous Pamplona summers, and he knew the apparently central conflict: the woman and the bullfighter. But he never planned the chapters out with any detail. In fact, at the end of the Paris section of the first draft, he roughed out six chapters, only four of which covered Pamplona. He intended, for example, to bring Count Mippipopolous to San Fermin. The Count never made it; he was the victim of a barely planned novel. In fact, when you look closely at the novel's conclusion, you find a good many unanswered questions: where did Cohn go? What will happen to Brett and Mike Campbell? Was Pedro Romero corrupted by Brett?

As soon as we say that these questions are irrelevant, we

have admitted that Jake is the central character. We have also recognized that Hemingway has, almost in spite of himself, created a modernist novel in which the point of view controls both the action and the reader. As in Fitzgerald's *The Great Gatsby*, Hemingway's minor character "I-narrator" becomes the most important character because he is the moral register of the action. Brett's rapacious sexuality seems like the central issue. But, as we discover, Brett is the catalyst whose presence triggers the chemical reaction while she herself remains unaltered. Her sexuality creates the conflict for Jake between serving his passive need for heroic action and his equally passive need for erotic action. In both cases—Pedro's bullring and Brett's bedroom—Jake is a passive observer, not a participant.

The structure becomes the natural motion or flow of the events: one thing leads us to another with little apparent effort on Jake's part. As Philip Young pointed out years ago, the book seems so loosely structured on the surface that the reader misses much of the internal control that focuses the material. Not until Cohn forces the conflict in Pamplona is it obvious why the novel began with him. The tensions that build between characters are gradually allowed their full rein during the fiesta. Good manners finally give way to passion: the group that seemed like such "nice people" comes apart. As Jake notes (146), the tension within the group creates a feeling that there were things coming "that you could not prevent happening." The reader's sense of that necessity is another unifying force.

The most vital unifying force in the novel is the bullfight and its accompanying detail: the festival at Pamplona is the cause for the group gathering; their behavior during the festival produces the tension that forces the action; Brett's seduction of the bullfighter triggers the surface violence as well as Jake's loss of membership in Montoya's club. How the characters react to the ritual is another way of characterizing them: Cohn wants to place bets on the outcome of bullfights; Brett cannot take her eyes off Romero in his tight green pants. Without the San Fermin festival there could be no story; the bullring is the crucible that holds the action together.

Of course, the bullfights, which come laden with so many associated values, are more than a unifying force. They are first and earliest a pagan ritual whose sources are lost in prehistory. On the island of Crete, bull leapers performed daring deeds in the ring centuries before Christ was born. The bull, with his prominent phallus, was and remains the symbol of male virility. (When Hemingway first saw the dust jacket for *Death in the Afternoon,* he was horrified to see that the designer had neutered the bull.) As soon as we recognize that, the irony and significance of the man without a phallus wedding his identity so closely to a phallic ritual becomes blatant. What Romero's tight trousers emphasize is his own phallus, his sexual identity: the contest in the bullring (and out) is between male animals and its primitive roots are fertility rituals. The *riau-riau* music of pipes and drum, the bobbing dancers, the garlic wreath worn by Brett down cellar where she is worshiped by the dancing men, the inordinate drinking—all the elements of the festival are Dionysian revelry taking us back to ancient times before the Catholic Church buried the old religions, times when the renewed fertility of the earth and the fertility of its inhabitants were closely associated. The irony of this infertile and disparate group of revelers being led to a fertility ritual by a man without a phallus is too bleak for comment.

At another level that Hemingway emphasizes, part of the bullfight ritual is used metaphorically in the novel. When the bulls are unloaded, Brett and Jake watch their high energy level being calmed by the castrated steer whose job it is to keep the bulls from fighting among themselves. Brett enjoys the dexterity with which the bulls gore the helpless steer just as she enjoys the way men behave around her. The gored steer leans against the stone wall. "None of the bulls came near him, and he did not attempt to join the herd" (140). The bulls, we are told, are only dangerous when they are alone, or only two or three together. If one is detached from the herd, he would be quite dangerous. Bill says, "Don't you ever detach me from the herd, Mike." And Cohn observes that it is no life being a steer. Mike begins to needle Cohn about being a steer hanging about all the time, but we know that the real steer is Jake Barnes.

By this time the metaphor is obvious: Mike, Bill and Robert Cohn are three bulls who are dangerous to themselves and others if they are not calmed. Jake Barnes is the castrated steer whose main job at Pamplona is to keep the men from fighting with each other. While watching the bulls, Brett observed that they used their horns the way a boxer uses his left and right punch. Early on we are told that Robert Cohn was an amateur boxer in college. Thus it is no surprise when Cohn's anger becomes so unbearable that he turns on Jake, the steer, and hits him three quick times just as the bull gored his pacifier.

At still another level, the protocol and pageantry of the festival provide a kind of order in Jake's world that is growing increasingly entropic, chaotic. No matter how disjointed his life has become since the war, Jake can count on the San Fermin festival to begin each year on the sixth of July. Whatever else might change, no matter how much flux disrupts the patterns of his life, Jake can rely on this week of festivity to remain like a rock in moving water. Each part of the disorderly ritual is important to this sense of order: what looks totally chaotic is actually on a schedule: the unloading of the bulls, the procession of San Fermin, the running of the bulls, the detailed ritual of the bullfight itself. If nights do not end and people do not sleep, if they drink too much and dance in the streets, that is all scheduled, all part of the order.

At the heart of San Fermin, which is the novel's heart as well, is the bullfight itself, lending its dignity to a less than dignified story. Within the ordered chaos of the festival, the bullfight is absolute order and decorum, total design. Within the prescribed ritual, the individual artist may, by his own will, find courage, purity of line, and grace under pressure. Dressed so gaudily in the face of death, the bullfighter takes real risks in a contrived ritual, testing his courage before the audience. He is their representative. As Hemingway said in *Death in the Afternoon* (1932), "It is the only art in which the artist is in danger of death and in which the degree of brilliance of the performance is left to the fighter's honor."

Pedro Romero never falters before the bull, seldom jerks awkwardly, never loses heart. Thus he becomes the one character in the novel whose values sustain him in the face of death. We see him perform with excellent bulls and an awkward one. The bulls do not matter. He is a professional whose pride will not let him perform at less than his best. On the last day of the festival Romero performs at the height of his abilities while bearing the bruises from Cohn's beating. He is and remains undefeated by Cohn, by fear, by death in the ring. His art sustains him. That is the key to Hemingway's devotion to the bullfights, as well as to their importance in the novel. No other character has a set of values that govern his behavior in the face of death or allow him to perform well in public places. But I do not think Hemingway means for us to emulate Romero; the point is not to idolize bullfighters. The point is that here at least one can find sustaining values in a world where so many other values have lost their currency. Romero is not a code character teaching his values to a younger novice. He is simply an example that all is not lost.

The strength of Pedro's role is, perhaps, residual from Hemingway's initial idea of the corruption of a bullfighter. Pedro becomes Jake's surrogate for heroic action in the bullring, and in a truly perverse way, Pedro again acts as Jake's surrogate in Brett's bedroom. But no matter how admirable Pedro Romero becomes in the reader's eyes, he is never the central character because Hemingway never lets the reader get close enough to Romero for that role to develop. When in doubt in a Hemingway story or novel, look to the end. There the reader usually finds that Hemingway has focused him clearly on the central issue. As *The Sun* goes down, we are in Madrid with Jake and Brett discussing what a fine life they could have had together. We are focused clearly on Jake's condition, which has produced the ironic but sad story we have read.

Like many of his generation who went to the Great War, Jake Barnes is no longer capable of fervent belief, religious zeal, heroic action, or satisfactory sexual relations. Robert Cohn may still throb to the romantic values of an earlier era, but he has no place in modern times. Pedro Romero, with his youth, skills, and blind bravery, is a throwback who could never function as bravely in Paris as he does in the bullring. Neither Cohn nor Romero are viable models for behavior. Cohn is too sentimental and Romero too remote. Neither Jake nor the reader can become a bullfighter, no matter how much we admire young Romero. In the bullring, Romero is sustained in his art by a code of behavior that he has inherited out of the past: courage, control, timing, balance, and pride in his art. But the skills of the bullring do not translate easily into our daily lives. Jake and the reader are left without behavioral guidance. Unless we learn easily by negatives on how not to behave, it is difficult to construct from Jake's experience how he should behave in order to make himself less vulnerable. Thus does the motion of the book take us back to the beginning, with the characters no better off than when we first met them. For most, nothing has changed. Brett is still Brett; Cohn, wherever he has gone, remains Cohn. They have not learned anything from the action. Only Jake is left more diminished than when he began.

In what seems to be a loosely constructed novel, Hemingway employs a number of devices to achieve his final unity. The most obvious device is repetition: everything happens twice, and the second time around it sets up ironic echoes. One example is the bar conversation between Jake and Cohn early in the novel (37–39). At Wetzel's over beer, Jake tells Cohn details about Brett's life, details Cohn has asked for but does not really want to hear: her two loveless marriages. Cohn tells Jake not to insult her, to which Jake replies "Oh, go to hell." Angry, Cohn tells Jake, "You've got to take that back." Jake thinks he means the remarks about Brett, but it is the "going to hell" part that Cohn wants retracted. Jake retracts, "Oh, don't go to hell," but does not understand Cohn's oversensitive response to what was meant to be a casual comment. Later at Pamplona before the fishing trip, Bill decides that Cohn is insufferable and "can go to hell" (102). When Jake reunites with Brett and Mike in Pamplona, he asks Cohn, "Where the hell have you been?" (134). Once again during the bullfights, Bill says "to hell with" Cohn. Jake replies, "He spends a lot of time there" (162). This string of infernal references culminates in Pamplona when Brett goes off with Romero. As Cohn insists that someone tell him where Brett is, he is told four times—twice by Mike and twice by Jake—to "Go to hell!" (190). Cohn explodes, knocking Jake down with one blow and hitting him twice more as he tries to get up. This is the scene that Hemingway was preparing us for back at Wetzel's, where Cohn wanted to hit Jake for insulting him. At Pamplona, Jake knows how Cohn responds to the phrase, knows which button to push to force the issue.

Unconsciously the reader picks up these repetitions, associating certain images with individual characters. We can watch Hemingway using the taxi almost as an appendage of Brett Ashley. The first time we meet her, Brett is getting out of a taxi (20). Later that evening she and Jake leave together in a taxi. When Brett returns from San Sebastian and her interlude with Robert Cohn, Jake meets her accidentally on the street: "A taxi passed, some one in it waved, then banged for the driver to stop. The taxi backed up to the curb. In it was Brett" (74). Using the same kind of terse, periodic sentence with which he first introduced her—"With them was Brett." (20)—Hemingway's style forces the reader to take notice. We remember Brett getting in and out of taxis and are not surprised when the novel ends with Brett and Jake in a Madrid taxi.

Some of the repetitions Hemingway builds into thematic

signs whose function will be discussed in a later chapter, but we should, at least, note them in passing. Most obviously, Hemingway repeats the image of bathing, associating it with both Jake and Brett. Brett and the Count disturb Jake as he bathes in his Paris flat. When Brett returns from her San Sebastian affair with Cohn, she tells Jake and Bill she simply must bathe. Later Cohn insists that he never went into the water at San Sebastian. At Pamplona Jake, drunk and defeated, tries vainly to get the hot water to run into the deep tub. When the fiesta finishes, Jake goes alone to San Sebastian to bathe in the cool sea, trying vainly to wash away the moral grime accumulated during the week of San Fermin.

Beneficial water, of course, takes on religious significance, and we should include among the bathing scenes the two references to Lourdes, the place in France where the Virgin Mary appeared to Bernadette. On this spot miraculous healing waters sprang forth to which ailing pilgrims to this day bring their physical difficulties. Outside the shrine resides a pile of discarded crutches and other medical aids, abandoned by those miraculously cured. The first time we hear of Lourdes in *The Sun,* Jake is sitting uneasily with Robert Cohn and Frances Clyne while she surgically dissects Cohn's character without benefit of anesthetic. Her voice drips with sarcasm as she explains to Jake why Robert has decided not to marry her: "It's just come to me. They've sent it to me in a vision in the Café Select. Isn't it mystic? Some day they'll put a tablet up. Like at Lourdes" (51). The next time we hear of Lourdes, Jake and Bill cannot get a lunch seating in the dining car because American pilgrims to Lourdes have booked all the spaces. The irony of Jake's crossing paths with Americans bound for Lourdes will be discussed later; for the moment suffice it to note that Frances's early remark about Lourdes sets up the word in our mental matrix preparing us for the second usage. Do that enough times with enough images and a sense of unity is achieved without following traditional structural devices.

In passing, we might further note that Lourdes was not a strained reference in 1926. During the summer of 1925, when Hemingway was writing the book, thousands of religious pilgrims crowded special trains to Lourdes, for on 14 June of that summer the Pope declared the peasant girl, Marie Bernadette, a saint. Later in his career, Hemingway insisted that symbols in his work were not like raisins in a loaf of bread; he did not simply stick them into his fiction. If there were symbols, they arose naturally out of the fiction's environment. His use of Lourdes is in keeping with his self-analysis: the public interest in Lourdes brought it quite naturally to Frances Clyne's lips at the Select, just as the Lourdes pilgrims are quite naturally on the southbound train carrying Jake and Bill to Spain.

In similar fashion, Hemingway uses the ever-present Catholic Church as a recurring, but natural image arising out of the setting. Wherever one looks in Spain there is a Catholic church at the end of the vista. A tour of the Prado art museum brings a deluge of religious art. Throughout Western Europe the Catholic faith remains visible, but in Spain it truly dominates. Jake tells us that he is a "rotten Catholic," preparing us for his church visits in Spain. These religious excursions do not provide the spiritual solace that Jake seeks, but repetition emphasizes his need. The final twist to repeated religious imagery comes at the end in Madrid when Brett insists that not being a bitch is what she has rather than God. Jake remarks that some people have God quite a lot, but does not say that he does. Brett replies that God never worked well with her (245).

Another repeated motif is the continual paying of bills. The importance of repetition beyond unity will get full coverage later, but we should note how the bills, as Jake reminds us, always come, and how frequently Jake pays them: he pays for bar tabs, meals, taxis, and tips. He leaves Georgette money to get home on and, later, makes sarcastic comments about the French attitude toward tipping. Bills that Jake pays are closely associated with the "nice friends" he has, another repeated phrase whose ironic impact increases with each use. At her supper with Jake, Frances Clyne forces herself on Georgette, telling her that Paris is dirty but it does have "nice people" in it. Georgette turns to Jake and says, "You have nice friends" (19), meaning, of course, that she finds them dull and boring. A bit later, Robert Cohn confesses to Jake that he is Cohn's "best friend." "God help you," Jake thinks to himself (39). At Pamplona after Bill has torn Cohn's character apart, he tells Jake that the funny thing is that Cohn is "nice." "He can be damn nice," Jake replies (101). Jake's *nice friends* gather in Pamplona where Montoya can forgive a man with *aficion* almost anything, even friends like these. In their last group meal before the fiesta begins, Jake senses the tension, and he drinks until he loses his disgusted feeling. "It seemed they were all such nice people," he tells us (146). Jake's sarcasm and irony pile up in the novel, creating a unified point of view and giving unity to the action's flow.

So many of Hemingway's repeated images come together in Madrid that they would provide a unity to the most disparately written novel. As we've seen, church and taxi images appear at the conclusion. We should note that the most apparent repeated image—drinking—is most conspicuous at Botin's where five bottles of wine are consumed on top of earlier Martinis. Brett tells Jake he does not need to get drunk, and he replies, "How do you know?" (246). All the drinking—social drinking in Paris, cooled bottles of wine on the Irati river, botas in Pamplona—comes together in Madrid where Jake must get drunk in order not to think about his less than admirable situation.

In Madrid, also, is repeated for the final time the ritual meal, of which there are several in the novel. In Paris, Bill and Jake shared tasty fare at Madame Lecomte's to celebrate their reunion: old friends together again in the good place. With typical Hemingway advocacy of the direct detail, we are told the menu: roast chicken, new green beans, mashed potatoes, salad, apple pie and cheese—Americans in Paris eating a typical American meal in a restaurant that has recently been included on the American Women's Club list of places to dine. On the train south, Bill and Jake are denied a meal in the diner, but at Bayonne they share a breakfast with Robert Cohn. At Burguete, the two fishermen feast on soup, fried trout, stew, and wild strawberries, all accompanied by much wine. At Pamplona before the fiesta begins, the entire crew—Jake, Bill, Mike, Brett, and Robert Cohn—after a drunken afternoon have their only group meal at the hotel (146). At Botin's, which Jake tells us is one of the best restaurants in the world, Brett and he share roast suckling pig and Spanish wine, but the ritual meal, like other rituals in the novel, has lost its power to bind people together. Jake gets drunk and morose; Brett babbles. On its surface, this conclusion in Madrid seems understated and almost maudlin, resolving nothing. But so many of the novel's repeated images come together here: paid bills (Romero at the hotel, Jake at the restaurant) ritual meals, too much wine, discussion of God, and a last taxi ride. The effect of these multiple and repeated signals is to tell us that the story is ending. The novel may have begun a bit irregularly, but, as experienced moviegoers, we recognize the finale. Nothing has been resolved, but a kind of unity has been achieved.

6 Geography and History

If the story is a sad one, if Jake does participate knowingly in his own disgrace, if the other characters have so few redeeming values, then why does *The Sun Also Rises* continue to intrigue readers? Why do they come away from the book feeling good about Paris and Pamplona? Why do they use the book as a tourist guide when they go abroad? Have they misread the book completely?

The answers to all of these questions reside in Hemingway's extraordinary ability to create the ambiance of a special time and place. When Jake walks "down the Boulevard to the rue Soufflot for coffee and brioche" (35), we walk with him and agree that it is a fine morning. If we have been to Paris, then the flower women coming up from the market, the students on their way to the Sorbonne, the buses on the boulevards all ring true. If we have not been to Paris, of course we want to go there even before reading this novel. Everyone wants to go to Paris. Jake's ambles along the boulevards serve to increase our appetite, and we walk with him past the men with jumping frogs and toy boxers, and with him we follow the man "pushing a roller that printed the name CINZANO on the sidewalk in damp letters" (35).

As any astute tourist can attest, the streets of Paris are this very day no less various and interesting. The writing room at the Crillon Hotel has been converted into a boutique, but the grand hotel remains as it was, looking out on Place de la Concorde. One can still follow Jake's various walks to many of the same bars and brasseries, for *The Sun Also Rises* is street-map accurate: every street, monument, and building is exactly where Jake tells us it is. An anise today at the Dome, the Cupola, or Deux Magots tastes no different from that sipped by Hemingway's fictional characters. That kind of accuracy accounts for much of the novel's effect on its readers. One does not have to approve of Jake Barnes and company to admire the view, enjoy the wine, and appreciate the street life of Paris.

The same is true for Jake's description of his Spanish journey, which is even more delicious than Paris, particularly to the very young who still have the stamina for a week in Pamplona without sleep. Each summer on the sixth of July the Festival of San Fermin begins as it has always begun with the rocket going up and the running of the bulls down the narrow, cobblestone streets to the Plaza de Torros. This summer they run past the bronze bust of Ernest Hemingway that was not there during Jake's summer, but for the tourist, little else has changed in the passing years. The *riau-riau* dancers still leap in the streets to the call of flute and drum; the botas of red wine still flow freely. The plaza is still dusty, and the Iruna bar remains the place to be on a hot afternoon. Montoya's hotel, which was Hotel Quintana, is no longer there, but with so many small, cheap hotels and so much inexpensive rioja wine, next summer's tourist will not miss one hotel.

We do not have to approve of or admire the amoral lives to enjoy the scenery and drink at the bar. Hemingway's talent for selecting the important and abiding details has created an interesting tension in the reader. The sad story set in the beautiful country sets up two disparate and simultaneous responses in the reader, valid responses which do not cancel each other out. When Bill and Jake hike through the beech wood above Burguete where the roots bulk above the ground and the branches twist and the sunlight comes through the leaves of the old, large trees in patches, we can agree with Bill: "This is country" (117). When the simple food and the country wine are on the table at Burguete, the reader is not concerned with the sadness of the story. And when the cold night wind comes down the mountains from Roncesvalles, we and Jake both can say, "It felt good to be warm and in bed" (111). At the novel's end, Jake cannot go back to Pamplona but we can. Our membership remains intact. The country is always there—in the fiction and in reality with no appreciable difference between them.

When Hemingway's friend Nathan Asch first read *The Sun Also Rises,* he told Hemingway that it was a travel book. As Robert O. Stephens has demonstrated in *Hemingway's Nonfiction* (1968), Hemingway was a skilled manipulator of the travel writing genre. He practiced it in his feature writing for the Toronto *Star* (1922–24) and returned to the genre at various points in his long career. More to the point, Hemingway was adept at using the techniques from travel writing in his fiction. Stephens noted: "Moving about Spain as an *aficionado,* he [Hemingway] learned about good cafés, pleasant hotels, breathtaking landscapes, famous paintings, eccentricities of people from diverse provinces, the places to get the best paella and to see the most handsome women, and the ritual to follow during the day of the bullfights to make the events of the arena the climax of a perfectly arranged day" (68). Asch was right about the novel, for these travel writing characteristics are responsible for a good deal of *The Sun*'s impact.

Much of the novel's narrative line develops while the characters are drinking at sidewalk cafés or eating meals. In the process the reader assimilates information of the sort he might have found in a travel guide to Paris. For example, at the end of the opening chapter, Jake tells us that he dined one night with Robert Cohn and Frances Clyne "at l'Avenue's and afterward went to the Café de Versailles for coffee" (6). In a period *Baedeker's Paris* (1924), the tourist could have been directed to 3 Rue du Depart where Lavenue's was recommended not only for its food but also for its noted wine cellar. Café Versailles, where the three have coffee and *fines,* was less than two blocks away on Rue de Rennes. It was not necessary that Hemingway tell us the names of the restaurants; nameless they would have served just as well for his narrative purpose. Naming them accurately was important to him as a writer. If he learned nothing else from Joyce, who checked every distance and place-name in Dublin for accuracy, Hemingway learned that the details must be true for the chemistry of the fiction to be convincing. This is part of Hemingway's technique in achieving what he called "the way it was": real restaurants and cafés on actual streets within an easy walk of each other.

This kind of savory surface detail runs effortlessly throughout the novel. The list of restaurants, cafés, and brasseries in the opening chapters was an accurate guide to where people like Jake and Brett might be found eating and drinking in 1925 Paris: Café Napolitain (13), Foyot's (16), the Select (27), Lavigne's and Closerie des Lilas (29), Zelli's (33), Wetzel's where the hors d'oeuvres are good (37), Café de la Paix (40), the Café Rotonde, and the Dome (42). All the places were real, and the street directions for reaching them are included in the prose. Where Jake and Bill Gorton walk through the lovely Paris evening, we, too, can walk—up Rue du Cardinal Lemoine to Place de la Contrescarpe and past the Café aux Amateurs on to Rue du Pot de Fer and then south past Vale Grace to Boulevard du Port Royal until it becomes Montparnasse (77–78). What is more valuable than precise, correct directions, particularly in another country? Jake's narrative of his journey to Spain is studded with similarly accurate travel information. If we follow him all the way to Madrid, we can still enjoy the roast suckling pig washed down with *rioja alta* at Botin's where the eighteenth-century ovens continue to brown the baby porkers to perfection. All of which tells us what Jake Barnes values in life: good drink and good food at a reasonable price. We may not approve of his behavior at Pamplona, but we cannot fault his culinary tour guide.

During Jake's early conversation with Cohn, he suggests flying to Strasbourg and walking to Saint Odile. In 1926, when the novel was published, air travel was still a novelty that few had attempted. One could, in fact, fly from Paris to Strasbourg, but it is interesting that Jake talks about it as if it were familiar to him. His knowledge of where to eat and how to travel marks him as an insider, a professional who never has the kinds of travel problems that plague most of us who are merely tourists. For Jake Barnes the French trains and their schedules are no mystery. He understands their dining system of table settings and knows how to deal with conductors. Jake's geography is precise: he knows where towns lie relative to each other; he does not need to consult a map. With his fluent French and Spanish, Jake Barnes is a professional traveler, an insider who always has an edge over most of his readers. He is the traveler we would like to be.

As Stephens has pointed out, Hemingway "was a connoisseur of approaches to cities and ports" (74), a technique learned from travel writing that he used to good effect in *The Sun*. Look at his description of the entry into Pamplona (93) or into Burguete (108) for the detail and the way he moves us through the landscape and into the village. If one drives that same road today one can see the roofs of Burguete spring up just as lovely as Hemingway has Jake describe them. The old travel guides often told their readers exactly where to stand for the most sublime or picturesque view. Hemingway's landscapes and city entries use these skills he developed in his nonfiction to great advantage.

But Hemingway's "views" are more important to him as

the background than as ends in themselves. In his nonfiction, he specialized in sampling the sporting activities of an area as they were set against the landscape. For Toronto readers, he sampled the Swiss sport of riding the luge downhill at breakneck speed. He also told them how to fish in the Rhône canal. Later in *Esquire* magazine he took his readers marlin fishing in the Gulf Stream and hunting in East Africa. In his fiction, Hemingway was equally accurate and detailed in his description of sporting activity. In *The Sun,* Jake Barnes takes us fishing with him on the Irati river, where we learn where to dig for worms, how to fish, how to clean the catch, and how to break the sweet fern to bed the trout. We are given an advanced course in the art of the bullfight when Jake describes in loving detail every phase of the ritual. We see the unloading of the bulls, their run through the streets, the matador in his room, the grand entry into the ring, and the spectacle of the fight in slow motion. Details we would never have noticed as raw tourists Jake points out. We, too, belong to that small group of aficionados who recognize the skill with which Romero handles his half-blind bull. Earlier in Paris Jake went to the Kid Francis-Ledoux fight, but did not tell us much about it. (From the first-draft manuscript Hemingway cut out six detailed pages describing the fight.) After Pamplona, we are introduced to the six-day bike riders at San Sebastian.

These sporting activities, which Hemingway learned to describe in his nonfiction, serve a purpose beyond reader interest in this novel. It is worth noting that the prize fights, the bullfights, and the bike races are spectator sports. Jake Barnes is not a participant—neither in the sports he observes nor in the sexual confusion he narrates. Even on the Irati, Jake does not become deeply engaged with fishing. Bill Gorton wades out into the cold water where he catches large trout. Jake pin-fishes (fishing with a worm on a hook), catching six smallish trout before he quits to read and nap. The reader is also a nonparticipant, a detached observer, carried along by Jake's interests and his ability to describe their settings. Thus it is that Hemingway's skills as a travel writer allow us to be fascinated by the setting, the cafés, the food and wine, the views, the travel tips, and the sports without committing ourselves to the amoral value system at work. We can drink at the bar without advocating the particular life-styles of Jake Barnes and his friends. Hemingway's ability to depict "the way it was" overrides the "sad story."

That we can read the book at two levels simultaneously and remain relatively detached leads to another obvious point: these are not characters with whom we can identify. This curious condition is not a function of distant time; we are not detached because the conflict and characters have become irrelevant. We are detached because Hemingway has provided only two characters—both male—with the slightest possibility of promoting reader identification: Pedro Romero and Jake Barnes. For the male reader, Romero may be admirable but only in the bullring or Brett's bedroom, where the reader has little chance of ever appearing. Romero has honor, pride, courage, and art—traits that sustain him in his profession or when facing Cohn. They do not, however, translate easily into our lives. We admire and value courage, but it is unlikely that we will face a hooking bull on a dusty afternoon in Pamplona. We will be the spectators, not the participant.

Nor can we identify with Jake Barnes. His sexual wound is not the reader's only barrier, but alone it would serve. Any male reader who identifies with Jake Barnes would be loath to admit it. Certainly Jake has many engaging qualities: his ironic sense of humor, his insider's knowledge, his stoic acceptance of his condition, to name a few. But to identify with him would be to suffer with him his sexual incapacity, a less than thrilling prospect that this male reader would rather forgo. Moreover, by the novel's end an identifying reader would be sorely disappointed with Jake's debasing role as procurer. A sexually maimed war veteran who pimps for a sexually rapacious woman has little chance of appearing admirable for the general reader. Not in this novel. Not when Jake is telling the story.

Point of view keeps the reader detached, not continuously, but at the key moments. After putting the novel down, it is difficult to remember that it was a first-person narrative told to us by Jake Barnes. So often Jake does not mention what he is thinking or how he reacted to bits of action. He has trained himself to be the detached, ironic observer. He has trained himself not to dwell on his own feelings or condition, for introspection can only lead him to self-pity. The few times that Jake shares his privacy, he and the reader are slightly embarrassed. Alone in his Paris room, Jake looks at his naked body in the mirror and tries to reconcile himself once more to his fate. He tries to not think about his condition, but to no avail. His mind continues to work until we see him reduced to tears—a grown man crying himself to sleep at night. Usually Jake keeps his private thoughts, and thus the reader, at arm's length, for he does not want to think about himself. At San Sebastian, Jake sums up his situation: "Send a girl off with one man. Introduce her to another to go off with him. Now go and bring her back. And sign the wire with love. That was it all right." (239). We wait for other comments, but Jake's detachment becomes our own: we are forced into the spectator's role, for Jake Barnes will let us get no closer. Early in the novel Jake tells us that he distrusts people whose stories hang together. By that standard we should trust Jake, for his story is disjointed and awkwardly told, and he himself is unable to be absolutely honest with us. His dishonesty resides in his unwillingness to tell us what he thinks. What he says is trustworthy; it is what he omits that makes him one of us—a flawed human being.

Jake is, in fact, an antihero of a strange sort. With all of the clichés about Hemingway's macho characters abounding, it has become difficult to read the text he gave us. There is nothing macho or hard-boiled about Jake Barnes. Beyond saying he was wounded on a "joke front," he will not tell us what he did in the war. At Burguete when Bill wades into the cold Irati river to fly-fish for trout, Jake is pin-fishing from the dam: a worm on a hook is not macho fishing. In Pamplona, Jake does not run with the bulls nor strut with the male players. He stands on the sideline watching. The only time in the novel he takes forceful action, Cohn knocks him flat on his back with one punch. Jake Barnes is no tough guy. Like Frederic Henry in *A Farewell to Arms* and Nick Adams in the short stories, Jake is continually vulnerable, a man to whom things happen. In that sense his brotherhood with Huck Finn is reaffirmed. Although far less passive than Jake, Huck's river journey is a series of accidents into which Huck drifts unawares. Continually he must respond to crises he had little part in creating. Jake Barnes would have understood perfectly.

What Jake does not understand is the historical context in which he lives. How could he? The embryo can not tell the shape of his egg, nor can we see the air we breathe. But we, the readers, should have a better perspective on Jake's narrative than he himself does, for the novel accurately portrays a historical era that we can see more clearly than our own. Looking backward, we should be able to read the novel's anti-Semitism, for example, as a product of its times. When Mike Campbell is asked if Brett has any money to pay the Pamplona bill, he says, "She gets five hundred quid a year and pays three hundred and fifty of it in interest to Jews." Then he modifies the statement: "They're not really Jews. We just call them Jews. They're Scotsmen, I believe" (230). Mike's casual remark is British to the core, but it could just as easily have been said by Jake Barnes. Anti-Semitism was so prevalent in the American twenties that it was unremarkable.

Automaker Henry Ford and his Dearborn *Independent* tried to keep America vigilant against the threat he claimed the Jews posed not only to America but to Western civilization. The trumped-up anti-Semitic "Protocols of the Elders of Zion" were supposed to be the Jews' master plan for gaining control of the free world. Today the document seems absurd. In 1926, many "100-percent" Americans believed themselves threatened by a Jewish conspiracy. Their fears were heightened by the resurgent Ku Klux Klan whose membership doubled during the decade.

In 1925 in broad daylight, 50,000 clansmen paraded down Pennsylvania Avenue in Washington, D. C. By the mid-twenties anti-Semitism was so rampant on college campuses that the president of Harvard presented a quota plan to spread Jewish students thinly to campuses across the country. The Harvard plan for Jewish integration was never accepted, but on more than one American college campus the KKK was a student organization.

When Jake begins his narrative by introducing Robert Cohn, the first thing we learn is that Cohn is a Jew. For the twenties reader this was an unnecessary statement; the name Cohn marked him for Jew without explanation. Jake goes on to tell us how Cohn's nose was improved in the Princeton boxing ring; everyone knew that the stereotypical Jew had a large nose. In that uncomfortable scene between Cohn and his mistress, Frances Clyne, Jake tells us how Cohn gets rid of his obligation by giving Frances two hundred pounds—roughly a thousand dollars. Here is Cohn the Jew paying off his moral debt with money. Jake is embarrassed, but there is a part of him that enjoys Cohn's discomfort. At Burguete when Jake receives Cohn's three-word telegram, "Vengo Jueves Cohn," Jake says: "What a lousy telegram! . . . He could send ten words for the same price" (128). The comment cuts two ways. Jake implies that Cohn's Jewishness is somehow responsible for the meager wordage, but Jake also reminds us that he is the one who is always concerned about getting his money's worth, a supposedly Jewish characteristic. In Pamplona when Cohn wants to bet on the outcome of the bullfights, Jake sarcastically tells him that it would be like betting on the war. "You don't need any economic interest" (99). The implication, of course, is that money must be involved for a Jew to be interested. The ultimate irony will become more apparent when we examine the values inherent in the novel. For the moment, simply note the money references that pile up like the saucers at the Dome and Rotonde.

Jake, we must remember, has good reason to dislike Robert

Cohn, with whom Brett has spent a long sexual weekend at San Sebastian. Jake, who cannot have Brett, resents anyone else who can, but he particularly resents Robert Cohn. He controls his anger, but Bill says it for him: "Why didn't she go off with some of her own people?" (102). Mike Campbell, her fiancé, agrees: "Brett's gone off with men. But they weren't ever Jews, and they didn't come and hang about afterward" (143). None of the men is shocked by Brett's promiscuity; what they cannot forgive is her choice of a Jew. Throughout the novel, Jake's anti-Semitism so colors his presentation of Robert Cohn that the reader cannot judge the man fairly. That's part of the point: that's how we were in those days.

Some readers will want to use *The Sun*'s text to charge Hemingway with anti-Semitism. True or not, the charge is irrelevant to the reading of the novel. Jake Barnes is not Ernest Hemingway. To confuse the author with his narrator is to misread the novel and to relegate Hemingway's insights into his age to the same level as Jake's. Jake spends little time thinking or analyzing the condition of his generation: he's too busy staying emotionally alive. Hemingway, in contrast, has given us a portrait of his time so accurate that historians and social scientists quote from *The Sun Also Rises* as if it were a historical event. Part of the novel's truth is its accurate depiction of the era's dislike of Jews. Yes, Hemingway also made disparaging remarks in his correspondence, which is to say that he was a product of his age. It would be most remarkable if he were not anti-Semitic. Ezra Pound, T. S. Eliot, and Henry Ford were anti-Semitic. So was the nation that nurtured them. Ernest Hemingway is a historical result, no better or worse than the America in which he was raised. We should not, therefore, shoot the messenger who sends us over the decades such a clear picture of our national values.

As Earl Rovit saw so clearly in his *Ernest Hemingway* (1963), a further irony is Cohn's relationship to Jake. The man Jake spends so much time disparaging is, in fact, Jake's curious double. Both men are writers: Cohn has published one novel and is working on another. Jake is writing the novel we are reading. Both men pay their bills, and both are in love with Brett Ashley. Jake may have physically unrequitable passion for Brett, but it is Cohn she takes to San Sebastian to sate her own desires and because it might do the romantic Cohn some good. At Pamplona it is Cohn whom Mike insists behaves like a steer—"always hanging around"—but it is Jake who is the real steer, calming down the bulls, and it is Jake who gets punched out or "gored" just as the steers are gored by the bulls. At novel's close, Jake goes to San Sebastian alone to recover from the festival madness. When he swims out to the raft in the bay, he discovers a young couple laughing in the warm sun. Jake makes no comment, but we should remember that Brett and Robert Cohn were at this same resort beach earlier in the summer. Jake does not say the young lovers remind him of Brett's disappointing behavior, but he does not comment on many things that bother him. He leaves them for us to figure out.

That Jake's bias so clutters Cohn's portrayal is unfortunate, for Robert Cohn is potentially more interesting than we are likely to judge him. If Jake sometimes sounds like Huck Finn, Robert Cohn has more than one connection with Tom Sawyer. Like Tom, Cohn pays moral debts with money. At the end of *Huck Finn,* Tom Sawyer knows that Jim is a free man but keeps him imprisoned an extra few weeks so that the adventure will be greater. Without asking Jim, Tom knowingly risks the black man's life. Then Tom gives Jim forty dollars for being such a good prisoner, as if the money can compensate for the indignities Jim has suffered. The parallel scene in *The Sun* occurs when Robert Cohn pays off his mistress, Frances Clyne. In lieu of marriage, Cohn gives her money. Like Tom, Cohn has also accumulated his opinions out of books. Jake's earliest and most devastating critique of Cohn's character damns him for taking seriously W. H. Hudson's South American romance, *The Purple Land,* which Jake finds "a very sinister book if read too late in life." Cohn, we are told, reads it "as a guide book to what life holds" (9). The reader, at this point, should remember the comic opening chapters of *Huck Finn* where Tom Sawyer explains the rules of pirate capture and ransom—rules he learned out of books. The implication is clear: Tom and Cohn are incurable romantics of the worst sort. Later when Cohn professes to dislike Paris, Jake thinks to himself that he probably learned that from a book as well. The irony of Jake's judgments resides in his own reading habits: rather than fish on the Irati he reads a mystery story by A. E. W. Mason, and after a drunken evening in Pamplona he reads Turgenev's *A Sportsman's Sketches* to keep the room from spinning around. The Mason story about infidelity would have been more appropriate for Pamplona; the Turgenev sketches obviously should have been with Jake on the Irati. What should we make of our narrator who distrusts Cohn because of his reading habits while himself choosing inappropriate books? We readers must continually remember that whatever we think of Cohn or any of the other revelers, we, too, are getting our ideas of them out of a book whose narrator distrusts people who get their ideas out of books. The closer one looks at *The Sun Also Rises* the more the ironies compound.

The most obvious bond between Tom Sawyer and Robert Cohn is their shared romantic attitudes—attitudes no longer viable in the postwar world, attitudes that died in the muddy trenches between 1914 and 1918. Honor and glory have become meaningless words to veterans like Jake and Mike Campbell. Mike's anecdote about his war medals underscores the point: his legitimate medals have absolutely no value to him. Mike, like Jake, does not want to discuss the war, which is the implied cause of his alcoholic tendencies. Cohn is not "one of us"—he did not go to the war; he still believes in outworn codes of behavior. Like Tom Sawyer, Robert Cohn still believes that ladies should be treated deferentially, honored in their presence and out, and rescued from villains whenever possible. Robert Cohn sees himself as Brett Ashley's self-appointed defender and savior. Early in the novel when Jake tells Cohn that Brett has married, divorced, and is now engaged, Cohn replies, "I don't believe she would marry anybody she didn't love." Jake says she has done it twice. Cohn gallantly refuses to believe this of Brett. Jake tells him not to ask about her if he does not want the truth. Cohn says, "I didn't ask you to insult her" (39). Jake tells him to "go to hell," and Cohn tries to pick a fight. In his childish, romantic way, Cohn is trying to defend Brett's dubious honor with his fists just as a storybook knight might do. In Pamplona, Cohn forces Jake into a one-sided fight by calling him a pimp, striking back at the man who has imperiled his lady-love. In Brett's hotel room, Cohn beats Romero mercilessly until he becomes ashamed to hit a defenseless man any more: the code of honorable behavior. Cohn wants to shake hands; Romero, beaten but undefeated, wants to kill Cohn. Robert cannot understand: gentlemen knights should behave better than this. He tries to shake hands, as if this gesture would clear up everything. As he leans down to shake Romero's hand, the bullfighter hits him in the face. All the honorable rules of "fair fighting" that knights once followed in books are not appropriate guidelines for daily behavior.

That Cohn should take the lesson, but not learn it, in Spain is ironically humorous if we remember the two famous knights who created their legends in Spain: Roland and his heroic rearguard action in the year 778; Don Quixote and his hopeless fifteenth-century adventures that satirized romantic dreamers. It is not forcing the issue to bring these two knights to bear on the action, for Hemingway and Jake have made a point of introducing the theme. As Bill and Jake approach Burguete on the bus, they see "the gray metal-sheathed roof of the monastery of Roncesvalles." Jake spots it first: "There's Roncevaux." Bill replies: "It's cold up here" (108). If we miss the reference, we miss the point. The monastery at Roncesvalles lies just down the mountain from the pass where Roland and his knights stood off the Saracen army pursuing the retreating Charlemagne. Today at the pass a stone slab stands to mark the spot for all time. On a summer day when the cloud level hangs at a thousand meters, the pass swirls in fog. It is the bright green grass and tall pines and goat bells in the fog that one remembers, and it is as real as Roland will ever be again. "It's awfully cold," Bill says; and he is right. The demands of honor are indeed cold, and the age of knights is past. Roland's honor cost him his life and won him immortality, but that was in another time zone. For Robert Cohn and all the other distant relatives of Tom Sawyer, the times are not for romantic heroes: Cohn's outdated sense of honor and his knight's rules of courtly love have no place among the generation we call "lost."

For Hemingway to expose his misguided romantic in Spain calls up the ghost of Don Quixote, the aged knight who was so out of touch with his times. Cohn tilts only at metaphoric windmills, but he is just as blind to surface reality as Quixote, and like the Spanish gentleman, Cohn tries unsuccessfully to make the world conform to his view. However, Brett is no more worthy of Cohn's courtly love than Esmeralda was the high-born beauty that Quixote imagined her to be. Cervantes wrote his novel as a satire on those who continued the stories of knightly behavior as if the values were still current. The story got away from him: we laugh at Quixote but we never resent him. Hemingway's satire on his age includes his contemporary version of the knight-errant, but we readers are not as beguiled by Cohn as by the old knight. The narrator's sympathy is lacking, but the message is the same as it was in 1605: the values no longer work.

7 Values

Readers today, affected by the conservative mood of the country, find little to admire in *The Sun Also Rises*. Unlike the sixties generation who read the novel as a rejection of false values, today's conservatives condemn Brett's promiscuity and question Jake's drinking. For this generation the novel is a study in moral failure, and their reaction against the Paris-Pamplona life-style is perhaps closer to Hemingway's original intention than most realize. Those readers who want *The Sun Also Rises* to be a hedonist's handbook to unbridled night life and sexual extravagance misread the book as badly as Hemingway's mother did in 1926.

In her letter, his mother enclosed a review from the Chicago *Tribune* (1926) that underlined her objections: "Except for the fiesta, which is vivid and gross and impressive and worth doing, the book is concerned with such utter trivialities that your sensitiveness objects violently to it. . . . Ernest Hemingway can be a distinguished writer if he wishes to be. He is even in this book, but it is a distinction hidden under a bushel of sensationalism and triviality." Using the review as a springboard, Grace Hemingway berated her son for his apparent abandonment of traditional values: "It is a doubtful honor to produce one of the filthiest books of the year. What's the matter? Have you ceased to be interested in loyalty, nobility, honor and fineness of life?. . . surely you have other words in your vocabulary besides "damn" and "bitch"—Every page fills me with a sick loathing—if I should pick up a book by any other writer with such words in it, I should read no more—but pitch it in the fire."[1]

His mother's letter lay two months unanswered. Finally Hemingway replied as clearly as he could: " . . . I am in no way ashamed of the book, except in as I may have failed in accurately portraying the people I wrote of, or in making them really come alive to the reader. I am sure the book is unpleasant. But it is not *all* unpleasant and I am sure is no more unpleasant than the real inner lives of some of our best Oak Park families. . . . The people I wrote of were certainly burned out, hollow and smashed—and that is the way I have attempted to show them."[2] *Unpleasant . . . burned out . . . hollow . . . smashed . . .* his novel cataloged representative lives of his time, and each life he measured with a moral yardstick created in Oak Park. He carried a piece of that so-called Village with him throughout his life, but at no time during his writing career was it more noticeable than in his early years in Paris.

When Hemingway first arrived in Paris at Christmas of 1921, he was delighted, intimidated, and appalled. Life on the Left Bank, for which he was totally unprepared, galled his Oak Park morality. His deep belief in Theodore Roosevelt's virtues of self-reliance and hard work was offended by the crowd of pseudo-artists he found lounging endlessly in the now (and then) famous cafés. Soon after his arrival in Paris, Hemingway sent back to the Toronto *Star Weekly* a feature story that began: "The scum of Greenwich Village, New York, has been skimmed off and deposited in large ladels on that section of Paris adjacent to the Café Rotonde. New scum, of course, has risen to take the place of the old, but the oldest scum, the thickest scum and the scummiest scum has come across the ocean, somehow, and with its afternoon and evening levees has made the Rotonde the leading Latin Quarter showplace for tourists in search of atmosphere."[3] He goes on to mock the dumpy American woman admiring her hopeless painting on the Rotonde wall and to mock the overdressed American woman with her three paid escorts. But it was the Americans pretending to be writers but not working at their writing who most infuriated the young Hemingway. He was different: he had a job; he worked hard. Even when he seemed to be loafing he was actually collecting grist for his mill.

Three years later when he wrote *The Sun Also Rises,* Hemingway did not abandon his Oak Park values. If Hemingway's mother had looked more closely at Jake Barnes, she would have discovered a fellow Oak Parker beneath his defensive ironies. Like Joseph Conrad, whom he read and deeply admired, Hemingway constructed a test of values: he put a representative man of his own culture down in a foreign country to see if his values could sustain him when separated from his nurturing society.

One of the traditional values that takes a beating in *The Sun Also Rises* is moderation in drinking. Today's reader is usually skeptical about the steady and heavy drinking in the novel: no one could drink that much and still function. One response might be that the characters *do not* function very well, but that avoids the real issue. The important question is *why* do the characters drink the way they do. In Oak Park, where alcohol could not be made, stored, sold, or consumed in public, this fictional flow of alcohol was particularly offensive to Hemingway's parents. Their son, however, knew that the best families in the Village kept private bars and drank at home while supporting Prohibition at church and in the election booth. In this practice they were no better or worse than the rest of the nation.

When the Volstead Act went into full effect in 1921, America officially began its thirteen-year experiment in Prohibition. By 1933, when the experiment was repealed by constitutional amendment, most people agreed that Prohibition had been an enormous failure; no one was sure what had cost the government more money—the ineffective enforcement of the law or the lost tax revenues from legitimate sales. The law had not stopped the majority of Americans from drinking; it had simply turned half the country into criminals who spent their money with bootleggers and in speakeasies. One of the reasons for the hordes of American summer tourists in Europe was the easy access to alcohol. Between 1925–30, about two million Americans—one out of every fifty-five—visited Europe, and like Bill Gorton on his trip to Vienna, many tourists traveled immersed in a vague fog of alcohol. "American Bars" sprang up in Paris to cater to the American drinkers who each summer in the twenties trebled the 10,000 English-speaking residents of the French capital. Whatever their reasons for travel, the American tourists forced up the bar prices on both banks of Paris. The moral hypocrisy of Prohibition that so irritated Hemingway's generation produced exactly the reaction that Hemingway documents in his novel. By 1926 the cocktail had, according to H. L. Mencken, become an American art form.

Jake Barnes does not drink as excessively as either Brett Ashley or Mike Campbell, a confirmed alcoholic, but Jake's drinking should be understood as a way of not thinking about his sexual and moral condition. If, at the end of the novel, he gets drunk at Botins, he has plenty of good reasons, not the least of which is his own reprehensible behavior at Pamplona. Having pimped for Brett, taken a beating from Cohn, and lost his membership in Montoya's club, Jake Barnes needs those bottles of wine to hide behind. He certainly does not want to think too closely about his moral condition. But then neither did America in 1926, and Jake Barnes is a native son, an American born into a time and place not of his choosing.

If Jake and his friends drink too much too often, do not place the blame on Hemingway; he did not create the moral climate that turned drinking into an indoor sport, nor was he responsible for the sexual attitudes of the period. Edmund Wilson once called him the moral barometer of his times: Hemingway recorded the changes in the moral atmospheric pressure. Home, family, church, and country gave this war-wounded generation no moral support. The old values—love, honor, duty, truth—were bankrupted by a war that systematically killed off a generation of European men and permanently scarred Americans like Jake, who fought during the last months of the debacle. A nation's "blue-eyed pride," as e. e. cummings called the American Expeditionary Force, went to the Great European War to "make the world safe for Democracy." That was what they were told by President Wilson. They believed that they were chosen to save Western civilization from destruction by the barbarous Germans. Later Ezra Pound would characterize the American war effort with bitter terseness:

> walked eye-deep in hell
> believing in old men's lies, then unbelieving
> came home, home to a lie,
>
> . . .
>
> disillusions as never told in the old days,
> hysterias, trench confessions,
> laughter out of dead bellies.
>
> . . .
>
> There died a myriad,
> And of the best, among them,
> For an old bitch gone in the teeth,
> For a botched civilization
>
> *Hugh Selwyn Mauberly*

The war had not been about the future of Western civilization, but the American participants did not discover that truth until the postwar conferences proved that the dying had been part of a power play, part of international economics. The 50,000 dead Americans ensured that the multibillion-dollar Morgan bank loans to the "allies" were safe. In 1929 in *A Farewell to Arms*

Hemingway would say that words like "glory" and "honor" had become obscene through overuse. These words that had so moved the previous generation of Theodore Roosevelt seemed, in 1926, forever devalued. The loss was not permanent; however, no one knew that in 1926. Mike Campbell's attitude toward his war medals is symptomatic of the survivors: the medals awarded for what was then called courage have no meaning for him. The bits of colored cloth no longer represent glory or honor to Mike, but he is not responsible for their devaluation. Mike is just another war casualty still walking.

If the novel's characters seem less than admirable, if their moral values appear bankrupt, so did their world appear, both in America and abroad. *The Sun Also Rises* is not a guide to reasonable behavior. It is not a song in praise of the so-called lost generation. It is a thorough moral examination of its time. If the results are offensive, we can not blame the doctor who conducted the exam.

If, like Hemingway's mother and Robert Cohn, the reader does not approve of Brett Ashley's rather random sexual activity, it is just possible that neither Jake nor Hemingway wanted approval for her promiscuity. Like Jake and Mike Campbell, Brett Ashley is another war cripple, for whom the stable prewar values have disappeared. When Cohn asks Jake about her, Jake tells him she is a thirty-four-year-old drunk whose "true love" died from dysentery during the war and who has twice married and divorced. This is the same lady who will not go to Biarritz with Count Mippipopolous for ten thousand dollars, but who will go to San Sebastian with Cohn for a week because it amuses her. Neither decision is complicated by the moral values that sustained the generation of Hemingway's parents. These were modern times, the first sexual revolution of the twentieth century. Everyone was "doing it, doing it," as the song said.

Nothing was quite the same after the war. Skirts rose from the ankle to the knees and a little beyond. Corsets disappeared just in time for Henry Ford's automobiles to put courtship on wheels. Girls as prim as Hemingway's sisters bobbed their long hair, rolled their stockings to mid-thigh, smoked in public, and danced all night to the jazz music their parents thought was corrupting the country. In 1919 the country began keeping statistics on the incidence of venereal diseases. Before the war, one did not speak of syphilis or gonorrhea, but the troops in France, who did not spend all of their time in the trenches, contracted various social diseases at an alarming rate. Before the men could go home to wives and sweethearts, they had to spend two weeks in debarkation camps to be checked for venereal disease, which had no easy cure in those days before penicillin's discovery. Between 1919 and 1926, when men were embarrassed to speak of the problem and many cases went unreported, the venereal disease rate in the United States doubled. The times, as a later generation would sing, the times, they were a changing. Between 1925 and 1930 over one million American marriages ended in divorce. By lowering residency requirements, Paris became the divorce mill of the twenties, where every year thousands of Americans took advantage of quick proceedings to shed mates. The year *The Sun Also Rises* was published, Hemingway's own marriage to Hadley Richardson ended in a Paris divorce; she got the royalties from the novel as her settlement.

It is in this context that we should read of Brett's promiscuity and Frances Clyne's affair with Robert Cohn. These are the "new women" of the period, the women who had been sexually liberated but who still depended on men for their identity and money. They are representative of the women who came of age with the movie sex symbol. They are the women of the first Freudian generation for whom it was mandatory to discuss sexuality openly. If Frances Clyne makes the reader as uncomfortable as she makes Jake Barnes, if Brett Ashley leaves us a bit irritated with her random sexual encounters, perhaps that is how Hemingway wanted us to feel. Perhaps he did not approve of these women himself. Perhaps he was telling his times as truly as he knew how: the usual supports that sustained the previous generation were no longer functioning properly.

Home and family—traditional bastions of moral guidance and emotional support—are inoperative in the world Jake Barnes describes. Jake himself is vaguely from Kansas City, but he never mentions his family. A few passing references to Brett's family and former husbands suffice: she's not going back to them anyway. Cohn gets money from his mother, and Mike Campbell is dependent upon home support to pay for his bankrupt habits, but neither man indicates that family carries any significant meaning for him. Nor is it likely that any of these characters will form a traditional family unit. Brett and Mike talk of marriage, but given what we know of them, we cannot place much hope on that union's permanence. Jake, of course, will never have a family.

Nor do religious beliefs sustain or give guidance to any of these characters. As we noted earlier, Jake is a nominal Catholic, but his Church has not been much help to him in coping with either his particular condition or with the world in which he lives. "Don't think about it" is the best advice he's been given, but that only works for him part of the time. He tries to pray but prays badly; he goes to confession but is not relieved. San Fermin is, we are reminded, a religious festival, but it is the pagan fertility ritual of the bullfights that dominates the week, and the chants of primitive *riau-riau* dancers drown out any religious sounds. On the two occasions when Jake might profit from a church visit, he avoids the encounter. At both Lourdes and the monastery at Roncesvalles—places where prayer has, in the past, been valid—Jake turns away. The pilgrims on their way to Lourdes cannot deter him from fishing at Burguete. He and Bill drink their bottles of wine in a parody of religious celebration (just as Brett in her garlic necklace down cellar in Pamplona becomes a pagan alternative to true religious worship). Later at Roncesvalles with Bill and the British fly-fisherman, Jake prefers to visit the bar rather than the monastery church.

No one else in the novel has even slight religious convictions. At the end, Brett, pleased with not behaving like a bitch, says, "It's sort of what we have instead of God" (245). Jake tells her that some people have God quite a lot. She replies that He never worked well for her. Jake suggests another martini. The barman / priest who presides over their Modernist Church of the Bottled Christ pours out two drinks. The parody and the ironic comment are complete. These characters may have failed God, but God's church has also failed them. Once important religious beliefs no longer sustain Jake or any of his friends.

The religion of work is also defunct in Jake's world. The strenuous moral and physical life advocated by Theodore Roosevelt no longer rang as clear or true as it had before the war. None of Jake's friends works: Mike Campbell and Robert Cohn both receive money from their mothers; Brett's money comes in alimony payments; Bill Gorton we do not know about. Like Montoya, the other clear-eyed analyzer of the human condition, Georgette, the prostitute tells Jake: "You have nice friends" (19). Her voice is heavy with irony, and *nice,* as we have noted, works as a pejorative in the novel. Hard work, that traditional American virtue that sustained Franklin, Lincoln, Edison, and Teddy Roosevelt, is temporarily out of fashion on the Left Bank of Paris. Jake is the only one of the "rotten crowd" who has a job, but even he tries to give the impression that he is not working at his journalism very hard.

At Burguete, Bill Gorton jokingly tells Jake: "You're an expatriate. You've lost touch with the soil. You get precious. Fake European standards have ruined you. You drink yourself to death. You become obsessed by sex. You spend all your time talking, not working. You're an expatriate, see? You hang around cafés." (115). Jake's reply—"It sounds like a swell life"—has a hollow ring to it. He may pretend that his job is not important to him, but his sense of who he is depends, in large part, upon his journalism. He saves his earned money to spend his vacation in Spain. He thinks of himself as a professional, one who sustains himself by his work, and he admires professionalism wherever he finds it.

Of all the significant characters, Georgette and Pedro Romero are the only two who practice their trade with any sense of professional dignity. No matter how difficult the circumstances, the whore and the bullfighter perform to the best of their ability. At the *dancing* when Jake has introduced her as his fiancée Georgette Leblanc, the prostitute plays the game. The fact that Georgette Leblanc was, in fact, a well-known Paris singer of light opera does not bother her. Perhaps she does not know. Even if she did, it would not bother her. If Jake wants to use her to insult his "nice friends," that's his business. She has her own business to take care of. Jake may not want her body, but he bought her supper; she gives whatever services have been paid for. Similarly, Pedro Romero, on the last day of San Fermin, gives the crowd a remarkable performance under difficult conditions. His face bruised and his body sore from the beating Cohn gave him, Romero works a difficult, half-blind bull not brilliantly, but perfectly (217–18). Most of the crowd do not appreciate his performance, but that does not matter: Romero does what he has been paid to do, not merely for the money but out of professional pride. The reader ends up admiring both Georgette and Romero because Jake admires them. Perhaps none of the central characters advocates the work ethic upon which Jake was raised, but Jake's admiration of it in practice should help the reader make the value judgments that Jake is loath to make.

We can, like Hemingway's parents, protest that Jake and his friends are despicable characters, or we can view them as products of a time and place, historical artifacts who tell us something about how we were in the twenties. Hemingway did not invent the conditions in which he lived; he did not create or subscribe to these values or the lack of them. Hard work was always central to his view of himself. He was raised on that principle and practiced it, at least in theory, all his life. Pick up his letters at any point and you will find him assuring someone that he is working hard. Whether he was writing or fishing or skiing, he was always doing it as hard as he could. Life was, for him, a competition: he needed to win, and he believed that hard work was necessary to win whatever the game happened to be. When the characters from Hemingway's mature years turn out to be hard workers all, it is not because he changed his tune. The tune was there in *The Sun Also Rises,* but it was played so softly and in such a minor key that, like Hemingway's mother, many readers did not hear it.

The only operative value in Jake Barnes's world is that of money. As Bill Gorton describes it: "a simple exchange of values." If, when reading the novel, you would put a dollar sign in the margin for every mention of money, you would see how central the exchange of values is in Jake's world. Everything has a price tag, and as Jake tells us in a voice dripping with irony, "The bill always came. That was one of the swell things you could count on" (148). With no other values to rely on, Jake can only assure himself that he has been getting good value for his money. He prides himself on knowing the best hotel, the best café, the best wine for the cost. Count Mippipopolous thinks nothing of sending his driver for a basket of Veuve Cliquot champagne; he can afford the price and the value is good. In such a world, moral issues are reduced to an economic question: can you pay the bill? That is the same question that Georgette is likely to ask, for Jake's world has been reduced to the level of the whore.

In chapter 3, with its remarkable juxtaposition of characters and themes, we first meet Georgette, whose brief appearance sets up the central issues of money and the price of the game. It is worth our time to look carefully at the chapter's action, which carries heavy freight. The first irony, of course, is that of the sexually incapable man engaging a prostitute to avoid his loneliness. Having picked up Georgette, Jake takes her to supper in a taxi where she makes an effort to excite him sexually. He tells her he is sick without describing his injury. "Everybody's sick," she replies. This seemingly off-hand comment will reverberate through the novel where most of the characters are psychically and spiritually sick: Brett's uncontrollable sexual needs; Mike's alcoholism; Cohn's hopelessly unrealistic romantic view; Jake's spiritual malaise. To paraphrase the chanting of a much later generation, "Hold them in your arms and you can feel their disease." This is the world of sellers and buyers, a world that Georgette understands and evaluates perfectly. When Jake tells her that his friends are writers and artists, she replies that some of them make money. As a seller she is only interested in money-bearing customers, and she understands the value of advertising her services on the boulevard.

Georgette's presence in the novel becomes important as an internal value system. When, later in the novel, scenes echo those from chapter 3, Hemingway is using simple sign language to make comparisons. For example, the taxi ride and the restaurant meal shared by Jake and Georgette will be repeated in reverse order by Jake and Brett later in Madrid. Hemingway wants us to remember the earlier scene, for it gives an ironic tone to the novel's conclusion while undercutting Brett's self-congratulatory dialogue. One need only watch the flow of chapter 3 to see Hemingway's intent. Jake arrives with Georgette at the Braddocks' *dancing*: the sexually disabled man with the whore. Brett Ashley arrives with a crowd of young men whose hands are white, hair wavy, "white faces, grimacing, gesturing, talking": the promiscuous woman with a band of homosexual men. Significantly, Brett recognizes that Georgette is a whore just as Jake recognizes that the men are gay. The homosexuals also spot Georgette immediately, and begin dancing with her as a kind of joke. Before leaving with Brett, Jake leaves a fifty-franc note at the bar for Georgette, telling the patron to give it to her if she asks for him but to save it if she leaves with someone else. He knows he will not see the money again, but the bill has been paid. This simple act will be repeated when Robert Cohn gives Frances Clyne 200 pounds (a thousand dollars) and when Pedro Romero pays the Madrid hotel bill when leaving Brett. As Bill Gorton says: "Simple exchange of values. You give them money. They give you a stuffed dog" (72).

This moral condition did not exist in a fictional vacuum; it was an accurate reflection of the world Hemingway had inherited. Jake's generation in the postwar world was the first to discover the joys of advertising and consumer credit. Technology, in the form of automobiles, phonographs, refrigerators, was available on installment payments. Advertising, as we now know it, came into full bloom mesmerizing the consumers. At Burguete, Bill parodies the high pressure ads of the day: "Coffee is good for you. It's the caffeine in it. . . . Caffeine puts a man on her horse and a woman in his grave" (115). The world of 1925 was filled with advertising and price tags. Anything could be bought. At the postwar conferences Hemingway covered as a journalist, he saw the futures of Europe and the Middle East being sold to the highest bidder. Every time he picked up the Paris *Herald* or the *Tribune*, he read about another American beauty marrying into money: Follies stars married sons of bankers—earning a quick return on their investments. At home Harry Sinclair had paid the Secretary of the Interior a bargain-basement price under the table for the U. S. Navy's Teapot Dome oil reserve: a simple exchange of values. Bootlegger money. Movie money. Quick money. The stock market climbed bullishly toward 1929 while car salesmen in Topeka and shop girls in Denver bought shares of inflated worth on thin margins. Everybody wanted a good deal, wanted good value for their money. With no other value intact, they were left with the values of the whore. Jake tells himself that getting his money's worth seems like a fine philosophy, but that in five years it will probably seem silly. Five years later (1931) the Western world collapsed in the worst economic depression before or since. The revelers in *The Sun Also Rises*, like their reading audience, were dancing toward that economic precipice without benefit of moral restraints.

When Brett arrives at the *bal musette* with her band of homosexual men, the policeman at the door looks at Jake and smiles. A recognition passes between the two men of the "otherness" of the new arrivals. That look says, "You and me, we're not that way." What the policeman cannot know, of course, is that Jake is in much worse sexual shape than the white-handed young men; his sexual decisions disappeared with his war wound. Then there is Brett, who does not look like a prostitute but often behaves like one. She and Georgette are sisters under the skin, as Kipling once said of another strangely matched pair of women—the Colonel's lady and Judy O'Grady. Brett may not charge a fixed price, but she is an expensive woman to drink with or sleep with. This scene passes judgment on Brett without ever saying a judgmental word. She is the sort of woman who would drink with homosexuals and recognize a prostitute. By the time the scene is completed, Brett and Georgette have traded places. As we leave the *dancing* with Brett on Jake's arm, we see the homosexuals have made a sport of dancing with Georgette. Irony is laid atop irony. What could be more ironic or impossible than a female prostitute dancing with a homosexual man? The answer is Jake Barnes leaving with Brett Ashley.

To bring the Georgette scene full circle, Jake and Brett leave in a taxi where Jake kisses her and Brett responds: "Don't touch me," she said. "Please don't touch me" (25). Jake's reply—"What's the matter?"—is what Georgette asked earlier. She puts Jake off just as Jake removed Georgette's hand from his groin at the beginning of the scene. Roles have switched and reversed: Jake is now playing the whore's part. When Brett says, "Don't we pay for all the things we do" (26), she speaks truer than she can possibly know. Their world, which once believed in abstract ideals and relied on moral behavior, has become little more than a diverse brothel where anything is permitted so long as the bill is paid.

The circle closes, and the irony is thick enough to be sliced with a knife. It is Jake's narrative, his story, but behind Jake is

Hemingway, the artist, manipulating the action. If he had truly wanted his readers to admire Brett and Jake, he would not have set up this chapter of skewed values. It is a sad story about smashed people whose lives are largely beyond their own control.

8 Signs, Motifs, and Themes

At the beginning of chapter five, as Jake takes us down the boulevard with him on his way to work, he notices three familiar street people: the man with the jumping frogs, the man with the boxer toys, and the man pushing the roller that leaves a damp word—CINZANO—on the sidewalk (35). While inviting readers to read these signs with him, Jake does not analyze them for us. One might say there is no need to analyze them, for not everything that happens on the surface of a novel bears significance: the street signs may be nothing more than accurate surface details. Yes, they are that, but streets are full of details, indeed so full that were Jake to tell us everything he saw on his way to work, the novel would get no further than that single morning. Therefore, these signs chosen by the author/narrator should at least be checked for significance, for of all the detail that Jake takes in on that particular morning, he has selected these signs to suggest what it was like on the boulevard.

Both the man with the jumping frogs (presumably toys) and the man with the toy boxers are selling their merchandise to tourists. Jake steps aside "to avoid walking into the thread with which his girl assistant manipulated the boxers. She was standing looking away, the thread in her folded hands." (35). Ralph Ellison thought this scene significant enough to use a variation on it in *Invisible Man*. Perhaps there is more here than Jake cares to comment on. First, one can say that selling and buying are a part of the novel: a simple exchange of values, as Bill Gorton says. The two pitch-men, we note, do not delay Jake any more than the three-card monte games on the streets of New York catch the attention of the streetwise. Jake is not on native ground, but he is not a tourist. That's the point. He avoids the unseen control threads, for he has watched the game plenty of times before. But the controls are there; someone is always pulling the strings. Like toy frogs, we jump to stimuli; like toy boxers, we respond violently when our strings are pulled. Throughout the novel Jake reacts to stimuli over which he has little control. In Pamplona his strings are pulled and he responds violently with Cohn, a trained boxer, who puts Jake out on the floor. Then at San Sebastian, Brett pulls his string with a telegram and he jumps to her aid. But here in Paris, Jake, the experienced man on the street, is not taken in or delayed by toys. Instead he follows the CINZANO sign the rest of the way to work. When one thinks of the effects of alcohol on *The Sun*'s characters, Cinzano, the staple Italian vermouth, may be an ironic and prophetic sign for Jake to follow.

For a sign to convey meaning, it must be read within a larger language that the reader understands. If one does not read Greek, the signs of Athens will mean nothing. If the reader of *The Sun Also Rises* does not understand that Paris prostitutes were required by law to be checked regularly for venereal disease, then he will miss the significance of Georgette's yellow card, the sign that she is disease free. The sign reaches our attention long after we watched Jake and Georgette in the taxi. There, when Jake told her he was sick, she replied, "Everybody's sick. I'm sick, too" (16). Not knowing at that point she had her yellow card, the reader was justified in thinking that Georgette was admitting to a venereal disease. Once we know about her yellow card, we have to reevaluate her "sickness." It is not sickness of the flesh but of the spirit, and in that sense, everybody in the novel is, indeed, sick. If we do not have the language framework for reading the sign of the yellow card, we never read her remark right.

The fault is not really ours or Hemingway's. Language continually changes: it is never the same river twice. Authors, writing for their contemporary audience, not eternity, rely on their readers' sharing a common language framework. Thus Chaucer used contemporary signs that his readers understood to characterize his pilgrims on their way to Canterbury. Today we no longer, unaided, recognize the meaning of many of Chaucer's signs. A wart on the nose, red hair, a gap-toothed smile—none of these signs means today what it did to Chaucer's readers. The same is becoming true for Hemingway's signs.

Today we have to explain more of them than was necessary when the novel was first published. In another hundred years, several pages of footnotes will be required to read the book Hemingway wrote. Examples from Jake's fishing trip to Burguete should suffice. Bill Gorton's apparently amusing conversation about "irony and pity" is a contemporary sign that no longer points to any clearly understood meaning. In 1925 "irony and pity" were current buzz words among the literary establishment. Their source was probably Anatole France, and they were a critical shorthand in New York where Max Perkins, Hemingway's editor, appreciated the satire. The average 1926 reader in Kansas City probably missed that sign altogether. Some things in books, Hemingway later insisted, were put in only for the amusement of other writers. Surely Jake's remark about "Henry's bicycle" (115) falls into this category. In the type draft sent to Scribner's, Bill's advice to Jake read: "That's what you ought to work up into a mystery. Like Henry James' bicycle." Bill was referring to the obscure rumor that Henry James had suffered an accident which had rendered him impotent. Charles Scribner's and Sons refused to print the statement, for they were James's publishers. Although the great man was dead (1916), his New York publisher still felt honor bound to defend him. Hemingway dropped the "James'," leaving the anecdote even more obscure than it began.

Other signs during the Burguete excursion are equally obscure today because they referred to topical events long forgotten. For example, when asked to say something ironic when asking the Burguete waitress for jam, Jake says, "I could ask her what kind of jam they think they've gotten into in the Riff" (114). No reader today can be expected to know about the 1925 guerrilla war being fought in the northern reaches of French and Spanish Morocco. Berbers, under the leadership of Abd-el-Krim, were fighting for their freedom against both French and Spanish colonial forces. By the late summer of 1925, the Spanish forces under the leadership of General Rivera were mired down in an unpleasant war with no end in sight. Jake's waitress is as unamused as contemporary readers for whom mention of a Riffian war is a meaningless sign.

It is worth noting that signs need not be words. Each day of our lives we read and sometimes misread hundreds of nonverbal signs. When Jake is returning to his rented rooms (29), he passes the statue of Marshall Ney where he stops to read the inscription on a wreath of faded flowers. Ney's statue is a sign that Jake understands; Ney was a heroic military leader who did his duty in a losing cause. Ney commanded the rearguard action during Napoleon's disastrous retreat from Moscow and rejoined Napoleon in his ill-fated attempt to regain power after his Elba exile. When Napoleon went under at Waterloo, Ney was executed for treason. Ney represents an earlier set of values no longer current in the postwar world that troubles Jake. Considering the debacle that Jake is about to be involved in, the Field Marshall's statue is an ironic sign for the reader who knows a little French history. This sign also says that Jake

Barnes knows enough to pause knowledgeably at the statue. Thus we have double signs: first the statue itself; then Jake standing in front of the statue. Each sign conveys meaning without explanation, just as everyday people convey meaning to us through appearances.

We speak of reading the character of a person, which is analysis of verbal and nonverbal evidence. Georgette, herself, is a sign who requires reading. Most of the foreigners at the *dancing*, particularly the Braddocks, misread her. They take Jake's irony seriously and treat the whore as if she were a respectable lady. Brett and the homosexual men read Georgette perfectly, and so does the landlord's daughter. At Pamplona, Brett and Pedro Romero have no difficulty reading each other's body language. When Brett wants to listen to Jake's confession, he tells her it will be in a language she does not understand. Literally, of course, it will be spoken in a foreign language, but Jake is really saying that Brett would not understand the concepts of guilt and forgiveness that Catholic confession entails. Afterward at the gypsy camp, Brett has her palm read in a language she does understand. That is, she understands pagan ritual but not Christian ritual. She is, by her own admission, "damn bad for a religious atmosphere" (208). There are plenty of signs to verify Brett's self-analysis. While the religious procession of San Fermin passes in the street, Brett is down cellar with a rope of garlic around her neck with drunken men dancing about her in pagan hilarity.

A more difficult sort of sign is the one that seems to read in a straightforward manner, or one that sounds familiar enough that we assume we understand it. In foreign countries, armed with a smattering of the language, tourists continually get themselves into difficulty by assuming that some foreign word has the same meaning as the American word which it looks like. The same sort of difficulty arises when we watch Jake Barnes balancing his checkbook (30). Because it is something most readers have done and because the figures seem familiar enough, we read past the sign without giving much thought to it. First, we should note that this scene follows hard on the heels of Brett's promise to meet Jake at the Crillon. "I've never let you down, have I?" she asked (29). Well, yes, actually she has in the past let him down, and as we know, she will continue to do so. In his room Jake balances his bankbook, now concentrating on money, the one value that he can count on.

We have no problem understanding that part of the sign, for the larger context that provides its meaning has not changed since 1926. However, those figures from Jake's American bank account bear closer inspection. He tells us that since the first of the month he has written four checks. Carefully he subtracts the four unidentified checks: the opening balance of $2432.60 becomes $1832.60. Without totaling the checks, Jake has given us the mathematical signs to conclude that since the first of the month he has withdrawn $600 from his American bank account. Given the writer's task of choosing details to inform the reader, we might ask why Hemingway and Jake included this detail. What does the sign tell us? First, it tells us that Jake has more money than he spends. He's not in debt. He's not dependent on anyone else to support him. Given the financial condition of Mike Campbell, Brett Ashley, and Robert Cohn, Jake's independence is important in characterizing him. The bank balance, in spite of the $600 expended, also tells us that Jake saves money—an American virtue in the Franklin tradition.

Another meaning is equally clear: Jake is not wealthy in the way that Count Mippipopolous is, but neither is Jake poor. But what we cannot say is how much that money is worth in 1926 terms. Of course, Hemingway's readers in 1926 had no such problem with the sign. Today the reader tends to register the figures in the framework of his own bankbook and today's money, which is to misread the sign. Some comparisons will clarify my point. This table is for American prices then and now.

GOODS	1926 PRICE	1987 PRICE
Flour (5 pounds)	$0.30	$0.79
Pork Chops (per pound)	$0.40	$1.99
Bacon (per pound)	$0.50	$1.99
Butter (per pound)	$0.53	$2.03
Potatoes (10 pounds)	$0.49	$2.29
Coffee (per pound)	$0.50	$2.99

Since 1926, the consumer price index and the wholesale price index have tripled. The average personal income has grown from $705 in 1926 to $3943 in 1970. In terms of today's dollar, Jake's six-hundred-dollar expenses would be closer to three thousand dollars.

But comparing American prices from two different eras is not the point. Jake was in Paris, not New York. Today in Paris, prices have risen to match New York prices. But in 1925, when the novel was written, American tourists flocked to Paris to take advantage of the incredibly low prices, for the exchange rate was twenty-five French francs to the dollar. At that exchange rate, a nickel bought a half liter of beer, and a furnished flat rented for forty dollars a month. In Hemingway's own feature story—"Living on $1000 a Year in Paris" (1922)—he claims that a decent breakfast costs about six dollars *a month*, decent suppers about fifty cents each. "There are," he wrote, "several hundred small hotels in all parts of Paris where an American . . . can live comfortably, eat at attractive restaurants and find amusement for a total expenditure of two and one half to three dollars a day."[4] In another assessment, written the same year as *The Sun Also Rises*, the author says that on $2500 a year in Paris one can live in a comfortable hotel, take tea at the smart places two or three times a week, spend winter in Florence or on the Riviera, and summer on the Brittany beaches or in Switzerland.[5]

Re-reading Jake's bank statement using the 1926 frame of

reference shows us how badly we misread the sign the first time through. Our narrator has spent enough money "since the first of the month" to support a more frugal man for six months. What conclusions can we now draw? One can safely say that Jake is spending more money than a single man in Paris needs to spend, but there may be mitigating circumstances. Jake is a journalist; he may have professional expenses that he's not telling us about. But we have no evidence to indicate that he has expenses at the $600 level. Looking at the habits Jake tells us about, we notice that he takes taxis without ever thinking about the bus or the metro. He buys drinks at the cafés and bars. On his night on the town, he treats Georgette to supper at Madame Lavigne's, which she says is "no great thing of a restaurant" (16). Sarcastically, Jake suggests that she can keep the cab and go on to Foyot's for dinner. Even at Foyot's, an expensive restaurant of the highest class, a modest dinner for two people would have been only two hundred francs, or eight dollars at the exchange rate. Jake is not an extravagant spender. During the rest of the night, he pays for three taxi rides, buys several drinks for himself and others, and leaves two dollars (50 francs) for Georgette. All around, it has not been an expensive evening for Jake who, as we have seen, prides himself on getting good value for his money.

When he returns to his rented rooms, we see only a living room, bedroom, and bath—nothing palatial certainly. What, then, is the point of his bank balance? An obvious conclusion is that Jake is not telling us everything about his life. I do not mean to suggest that Jake Barnes is leading a secret life, only that he is arranging his story, telling us what he thinks is relevant, stage managing the details. I do not think he is trying to mislead us: he is not an untrustworthy narrator. Neither is he a narrator who takes special pains to explain everything to his reader. If he picks up more bar bills than are his fair share, he does not feel compelled to talk about them.

Perhaps I am making more of this bank statement than it

warrants, yet there it is on the page for us to deal with. It seems somewhat extraneous; we do not need to know the exact figures. Given Hemingway's usual careful selection of detail, we are being tacitly asked to deal with this data in a sensible manner. We never will know what Jake spent his $600 on. There are no old bills to dig up: Jake Barnes has no life beyond these pages, which contain all the data we will ever have. The manuscript sheds no better light on the matter: what you see on the printed page about the bank balance is what Hemingway wrote in the blue exercise book on the first draft. I suggest, therefore, rather than directing us inward toward smaller supporting details to account for the spent $600, this sign directs us outward toward larger issues. Hemingway has placed a marker early in the text telling us to pay close attention to money transactions, for, in some way, they will be important to our reading of the novel. This conclusion reinforces what I suggested in the last chapter: money is the only value that has meaning in this cross section of the postwar world.

Money, of course, is not a moral value, being neither good nor evil; affluence or bankruptcy do not disclose one's spiritual condition. Paying one's bills on time is a social value, not a moral one. Nowhere in the New Testament does Christ advise those seeking spiritual salvation to place their faith in their bank balance. Jack the Ripper probably paid his bills promptly the first of every month. Would-be followers of Christ are advised in the New Testament to give their money to the needy and follow their Leader. And we all remember what Christ did to the moneylenders in the Temple. In this context, the point becomes clear. If money has become the only operative value for this postwar generation, then it is spiritually sicker than it knows. That is the wider truth toward which the sign of Jake's bank balance points. When the only criteria for moral behavior becomes "getting good value for one's money," then we are truly bankrupt, spiritually and morally.

In June of 1925, a month before he began writing *The Sun*

Also Rises, Hemingway read and praised *The Great Gatsby*, written by his friend F. Scott Fitzgerald. As several commentators have noted, there is more than a passing similarity between the two books. Indeed, when twenties historians quote from fiction, they almost always draw from both books, for each indicts a sick society that has lost its moral bearings. Fitzgerald's narrator, Nick Carraway, contributes to the formation of Jake Barnes. The two are both seemingly minor-character narrators who think that they are less important than the story they are telling. Both men are bewitched by a woman with whom they cannot have sexual relations: Nick by Daisy Buchanan, his cousin and a married woman; Jake by Brett Ashley. Both men act as procurers: at Gatsby's request, Nick arranges for him a clandestine meeting with Daisy; Jake, as we've seen, arranges for Brett her meeting with Pedro Romero. Both narrators are left alone at the end of their stories to clean up after the careless main participants.

Such parallels are not coincidental. Hemingway, who was competitive about everything, particularly writing, approached his novel like a challenge match with Fitzgerald. After breaking his contract with his publisher, Boni and Liveright, Hemingway switched to Fitzgerald's publisher, Charles Scribner's and Sons, where he worked with Fitzgerald's editor, Max Perkins. This change of publisher was carried out at Fitzgerald's urging, for he genuinely admired the young Hemingway, who seemed to be leading the active, uncompromising life that Fitzgerald saw slipping away from himself. Hemingway was flattered by the established writer's interest, and their correspondence for a couple of years is one of the funniest of American's literary relationships. Between the two of them, they anatomized the moral condition of America in the mid-twenties. Fitzgerald at home and Hemingway in Paris were taking the same pulse, hearing the same sick wheezing in the national respiration. Both writers focused on the same symptom: moral confusion in which money became the principal measurement. Daisy Buchanan's voice sounds like money to Gatsby, and the sound of money tinkles satirically through Jake's narrative.

When the slightly drunk Bill Gorton tries to get Jake to buy a stuffed dog, he tells Jake, "Simple exchange of values. You give them money. They give you a stuffed dog" (72). Throughout the novel Jake is faced with moments of simple exchanges of values: he gives Georgette a meal for her conversation; he pays for drinks, for food, for tickets; at Pamplona he exchanges his membership in Montoya's club to satisfy Brett Ashley's desire for Romero. All about him, money is a steady issue. At Burguete, Bill Gorton says jokingly, "One group claims women support you. Another group claims you're impotent" (115). Jake, as we know, is self-supporting, but Robert Cohn, Mike Campbell, and Brett Ashley are dependent one way or another on family support. As Count Mippipopolous knows, money buys affection, support, agreement, and service in an age when no other principles have survived the war. One of the nicer counterstatements to this cynical view takes place when Jake tries to tip the barmaid in a small Spanish town: "I gave the woman fifty centimes to make a tip, and she gave me back the copper piece, thinking I had misunderstood the price" (106). That, too, is a sign: a miscommunication; a conflict of two value systems; a reminder to Jake that not everyone is for sale.

At the end of the fiesta, when the group has rented the car to Bayonne (229–32), their parting is soured by the bill, which, as Jake told himself earlier, always came. Mike cannot pay his bar bill or his share of the car. Jake pays for the rental car. As Jake tips his way out of France and back to San Sebastian, his ironic tone of voice almost loses control: "Everything is on such a clear financial basis in France. . . . No one makes things complicated by becoming your friend for any obscure reason. If you want people to like you you have only to spend a little money" (233). When Brett calls him to Madrid, Jake finds that Romero has paid the hotel bill, in effect paying for his brief affair with Brett.

Adrift in a world with its moral compass broken, Jake makes do as best he can. He did nothing to create the "clear financial basis" for human relationships that surrounds him. In Pamplona, in one of his rare self-examinations, Jake told us: "You paid some way for everything that was any good. I paid my way into enough things that I liked, so that I had a good time. . . . Enjoying living was learning to get your money's worth. . . . The world was a good place to buy in. It seemed like a fine philosophy. In five years, I thought, it will seem just as silly as all the other fine philosophies I've had" (148). Five years after the publication of *The Sun Also Rises* was 1931, and America, along with the rest of Western civilization, was deep in the Great Depression. What Hemingway, through his narrator Jake Barnes, has carefully described are the careless attitudes of the generation that carelessly spent its way into the whirlpool. In retrospect, Jake's bank balance is a clear sign pointing toward one of the novel's central issues that even the most casual reader finally understands.

At the beginning of chapter 3 a more elusive sign appears that needs our attention. Enroute to their dinner at Madame Lavigne's, Jake and Georgette pass the New York *Herald*'s window of clocks (15). Georgette asks what they are for. Jake tells her, "They show the hour all over America." She replies, "Don't kid me." At first reading, this exchange seems to characterize Georgette as a less-than-sophisticated citizen who does not believe in foreign time zones. She is perfectly existential, living entirely in the present tense and, for that matter, in the present time zone. If the *Herald*'s clocks were the novel's only sign calling our attention to the problem of time, we might be able to ignore them. However, time references so proliferate that eventually one must question their presence.

These time references vary: some refer to time of day; some to day of week; some to the year. Many take curious turns that are sometimes perplexing. Some moments in the novel last longer than others. At Pamplona, Bill and Mike argue about how long the run before the bulls in the street lasted. Mike says it was fifteen minutes. Bill replies: "Oh, go to hell . . . You've been in the war. It was two hours and a half for me" (200). Duration depends upon the observer. At San Sebastian, Jake has to reset his watch, having gained an hour crossing the frontier (234), an arbitrary time line. Early in the novel Frances Clyne complains that no one keeps appointments punctually anymore. So when Brett promises to meet Jake at the Crillon Hotel at five the next day (29), neither Jake nor the reader is greatly surprised when Brett fails to keep the rendezvous. Throughout the novel, Brett is late. She is late getting to Pamplona and late returning, for she operates on her own standard time. No one finds fault with her failing, nor does she take particular notice of it. However, one way to read this sign would be the same way we should have read the *Herald*'s clocks: time is relative; it depends on where you are. Brett's time is also relative to herself: she arrives as she pleases, declaring her own time zone.

Brett's self-centered time is easily accommodated, but what are we to make of the calendar derived from the specific dates that Jake provides in the course of the novel? Jake tells us that on Monday, 20 June, he and Bill attended the Ledoux-Kid Francis boxing match (70, 81). In fact, Hemingway witnessed the fight himself, but not on 20 June. The real fight took place on Tuesday, 9 June 1925. Today no one remembers the fight or when it took place, but in 1926 some of the Paris readers might have remembered. Why would Hemingway have Jake cite the wrong date of a known fight? Furthermore, 20 June did not fall on a Monday in 1924 or in 1925, the only two years in which the action of the novel could have taken place. Later we are told that the San Fermin festival began on Sunday, 6 July, which would fit the 1924 calendar, but would not fit with the death of Bryan. Perhaps Hemingway simply made mistakes, forgot the correct date. It is not the sort of mistake he tended to make, but it is possible. But why even give us the exact date? It does not contribute to our following the narrative flow. There was no need to call our attention to the date, but, with Hemingway's approval, Jake gives us other specific dates in chapter 9. We learn that Jake plans to leave for Spain on 25 June (81), and that he does not see Brett again until 24 June. Why are we being given this information that seems to add nothing to the novel? Certainly the conflict is not dependent on readers knowing the correct date.

A similar piece of seeming irrelevant information is placed in the spotlight at the very end of the novel. While Jake and Brett are drinking martinis in Madrid (244), Brett remarks that Romero was only nineteen years old. A few lines later she tells Jake that Romero was born in 1905. "Think of that," she says. Jake replies somewhat laconically, "Anything you want me to think about it?" Brett tells him not to be an ass, and they order another round of drinks. But Jake's question needs attention: what should the reader think of this information, this sign. What does it say? That Romero was younger than Brett? We knew that already. That 1905 was nineteen years ago? Add it up: that makes the action take place in either 1924 or 1925, depending on when his birthday came in the year. Knowing *The Sun Also Rises* was published in 1926, the reader can now say that the action took place in one of the two previous years. But no matter how hard we try, we will not be able to make the novel's action fit into the calendar from either year. That is the catch and maybe the point of those dates at the end. If we follow the clues and construct the calendar, the dates do not work. Something has gone wrong with time in this novel, whose title assures us that the sun rises, that time is relevant to our reading.

If you still think this mountain looks more like a mole hill, consider the drunken conversation between Jake and Bill on their fishing trip. When Bill jokes about William Jennings Bryan, Jake says that he read about Bryan's death in the paper the day before (121). Bill then gives a funny oration about Bryan, aping the famous orator's inflated rhetoric and referring obliquely to the Scopes Monkey Trial in which Bryan was a principal defender of the fundamentalist law that prohibited the teaching of evolution in the Tennessee school system (122). This mention of Bryan's death seems to establish the novel's year as 1925, but it raises an even greater time problem. Bryan died on 26 July 1925, and as Jake points out in the opening lines of chapter 15, the fiesta of San Fermin began on Sunday 6 July (152). Since the fishing trip is before San Fermin, Jake has the great orator dying almost a month before his actual death. How could either Hemingway or Jake have made such a mistake? The manuscript shows that Hemingway revised this passage heavily; the first draft refers more directly to the "monkey business," but not until his revisions did Hemingway add the information on Bryan's death.

Another time reference during the Burguete interlude confuses the perceptive reader even further. Close to the end of the fishing trip, Jake tells us they had stayed five days at Burguete (125). The first draft of the manuscript shows the number as three, then four, and finally five as if Hemingway were trying to correct the skewed calendar. None of the numbers works. On the next page a letter arrives from Mike Campbell; dated Sunday, it says he and Brett will arrive in Pamplona on Tuesday:

> "What day of the week is it?" I asked Harris.
> "Wednesday, I think. Yes, quite. Wednesday. Wonderful how one loses track of the days up here in the mountains."
> "Yes. We've been here nearly a week."
>
> (127)

Nearly a week is either the five days Jake mentioned, or perhaps six days. But if the day is Wednesday, it should also be 29 June based on when Jake and Bill left Paris. But, no surprise, there was no Wednesday, 29 June, in either 1924 or 1925: the problem of days has multiplied.

No matter where you begin to construct a linear narrative for *The Sun Also Rises*, time falls out of joint: days disappear or multiply; hours stretch and shrink. At the San Fermin festival, time becomes irrelevant: Jake does not know what time he gets to bed (147); Cohn falls asleep and loses two hours (159); Bill and others are up all night and sleep to noon (161). For that week in Pamplona the only measurement of time is when the bullfights begin and end; the times of other activities exist relative to the central spectacle in the bull ring. It is not just in the mountains that one loses track of time in this novel, but what is the point? Why is Hemingway playing these time games with us?

The easiest answer is that he simply made sloppy mistakes. In learning about narrative construction on the job, he was not able to get all the joints to fit evenly. The biographical reader would say that Hemingway conflated two summers at Pamplona into one novel. The good fishing trip of 1924 came after the festival, not before it. In transposing the trip, he simply made serious calendar mistakes. Another biographical reader might say that Hemingway was so worried about libel suits that he deliberately constructed a time scheme that he knew would not fit either 1924 or 1925, the two years that contributed to the novel. But what do we make of the death of Bryan? He certainly knew when Bryan died, and he certainly moved the date. And why even give us the specific dates or the birth year of Romero? Why call our attention to specific time at all?

That question takes us right back to Jake and Georgette in the taxi passing the *Herald* clocks—the measurement of standard time all over the United States. "Don't kid me," Georgette said. What Hemingway did not say on the surface of the novel was that Albert Einstein would have agreed with Georgette: in the realm of his mind experiments there was no standard time. Time and space were relative in a universe whose only constant was the speed of light. In Einstein's now classic mental experiment, two men—one on a passing train and the other on the platform—each carries a clock and a measuring rod. The train moves at the speed of light; the man on the platform is stationary. As the train passes the platform, each man measures the window on the train. The man on the platform's measurement is shorter than the man on the train's measurement. The man passing at the speed of light measured a stationary window; the stationary man measured a window passing at the speed of light. Both measurements were relatively correct, but neither measurement was correct for both men. The length of the window varied depending upon the position of the measurer in time and space relative to it. Moreover, the two clocks appeared to run at different rates: to the platform observer, the train clock ran more slowly than the stationary clock.

"Don't kid me," you might well reply. Unfortunately the Newtonian world of standard measurements broke down in the early part of this century. In a quantum universe of probabilities, nothing is absolute, nothing certain but the speed of light. All else is relative. In March 1922, while Hemingway was learning his way about Paris, Albert Einstein was in town delivering a series of lectures. Einstein, whose first theoretical paper on relativity was published in 1905, had, by 1925, become a world celebrity whose picture needed no caption. His name and his ideas were bandied about in the popular press as frequently as they appeared in scientific journals. Between 1922 and 1928 the *New York Times* carried 172 stories about Einstein; during the same period almost a hundred articles about Einstein appeared in English and American periodicals. There is no evidence that Hemingway ever read anything that Einstein wrote, but the young author could not have avoided a general understanding of the physicist's ideas that had permeated the air of the twenties.

Let us look closely at the train station scene in Pamplona where Jake, Bill, and Robert Cohn are waiting for Brett and Mike to arrive (95–99). The three men are standing on the platform as the train pulls into the station. Cohn and Bill have a hundred-peseta bet on whether Brett arrives on time. Jake hedged, saying she would arrive but maybe not on time. Of course Brett is not on the train. Her telegram implies she might arrive the next day; Cohn waits for her; Jake and Bill leave for Burguete. Brett does not arrive until almost a week later. To stage this scene on a railway platform in a book where time is out of joint might suggest that Hemingway was having a bit of fun with Einstein's experiment.

Hemingway's point, however, is less theoretical than Einstein's and more straightforward: time simply does not have the same meaning to Brett as it does to Robert Cohn or to Jake Barnes. Jake has learned to accept her behavior. When she woke him up in the Paris night banging on his door, her appearance was neither questioned nor criticized. It was 4:30 A.M. and Brett said she "had no idea what hour it was" (32). While not moving at the speed of light, Brett does move at her own standard pace. Her erratic sense of time complements the erratic sense of values that has left this postwar generation to their own moral devices. There are no longer any fixed standards for behavior any more than there is a standard meter in the post-Einsteinian universe. In a novel depicting the loss of standards, it seems perfectly appropriate for time to be skewed.

There will be readers for whom a literate, allusive Hemingway does not match their inherited expectations of the writer. What these readers sell short is the milieu that nurtured *The Sun*'s rising and Hemingway's competitive nature, which turned the simplest activity into a challenge match. Shortly after Hemingway arrived in Paris in December 1921, he met Ezra Pound, Gertrude Stein, James Joyce, and Sylvia Beach. While Pound was corresponding with T. S. Eliot on *The Waste Land*'s final draft, Hemingway was a frequent visitor in Pound's apartment. When Sylvia Beach published Joyce's *Ulysses* (1922), Hemingway was one of the first and most enthusiastic readers of that experimental novel. In 1926, shortly after *The Sun*'s publication, Hemingway and Einstein were among the 167 who signed a petition to keep Joyce's *Ulysses* from being pirated in the United States.

Wherever Hemingway looked in those days, the new masters of his trade were playing time games: Eliot's poem fragmented time; Pound was launched on his epic time-voyage he called *The Cantos*; Joyce lavished his considerable skills on a single day in Dublin's life; and Gertrude Stein composed in her curious "continuous present" tense. By 1925, when Hemingway wrote his novel, his literate friends, acquaintances, and enemies were the leading edge of cultural change: Scott Fitzgerald, John Dos Passos, Ford Madox Ford, Ernest Walsh, Archibald MacLeish, Harry Crosby, Edmund Wilson, Joyce, Pound, and Stein. Nothing ordinary would be sufficient for readers such as these. Hemingway had his eye on the main chance, the wider audience, but for his own pride, he needed to write a novel that might amuse his heady friends. In *The Sun Also Rises,* he left us, his less creative readers, a sufficient number of signs so that we could follow his game and his meaning. The very title calls our attention to one of the few certainties that remained for that postwar generation: the sun rising on another day as disjointed as the preceding one.

A no less prevalent sign is the water, whose presence in scene after scene requires our attention. Count up the bathing references and see that *The Sun* is one of the best-washed novels you have read. In a bathrobe, Jake meets Brett and the Count at his apartment door: a bath interrupted. Perhaps not significant, but a beginning for the theme. Later, when Brett has just returned from her San Sebastian excursion with Robert Cohn, she stops Jake and Bill Gorton on the street (74):

> "I say I'm just back. Haven't bathed even. Michael comes in tonight."
> "Good. Come on and eat with us, and we'll all go to meet him."
> "Must clean myself."
> "Oh rot! Come on."
> "Must bathe. He doesn't get in till nine."

Coming back from a week of casual fornication with a newly met friend, Brett truly needs a deep cleansing before meeting her fiancé. The night after Mike Campbell arrives, Brett tells Jake again of her need to bathe (83). The hotel where Mike and Brett have registered is, according to Campbell, a brothel, a symbolically appropriate place for Brett, perhaps, but the least likely and most ironic place for a cleansing bath.

One might be reminded of T. S. Eliot's *Waste Land* brothel madame, Mrs. Porter: "O the moon shone bright on Mrs. Porter/And on her daughter/They wash their feet in soda water." In the bawdy song to which Eliot referred, it was a well-used part of their anatomy more closely associated with their trade that Mrs. Porter and her daughter so dutifully washed. Brett Ashley, indeed, needs just such a washing. To connect Hemingway's novel with Eliot's bleak poem of modern times is not as unlikely as it might seem. Remember that Hemingway read *The Waste Land* soon after meeting the poem's editor, Ezra Pound. In his own library, Hemingway would later accumulate all of Eliot's work, and he left allusive statements to the poem in *A Farewell to Arms* (1929) and *Death in the Afternoon* (1932). Like *The Waste Land, The Sun Also Rises* focuses on failed sexual relationships as metaphors for the postwar human condition. Both poem and novel use man's sexual inadequacies as a sign of his moral and spiritual failings. In the poem the land's fertility is not renewed by needed water, and the rituals no longer work. Similar rituals, both Christian and pagan, fail to restore sexual order in Hemingway's bleak view of modern life: neither the religious feast of San Fermin nor the pagan fertility ritual of the bullfights restore order. And in both poem and novel, no temptation is without its taker. Hemingway's use of Eliot's *Waste Land* as an informing context for his novel is not surprising. Scott Fitzgerald used the poem successfully in his "valley of ashes" section of *The Great Gatsby*. In 1926, with *The Waste Land* on every literate mind, no one could write a novel in which water and bathing figured as prominent signs and *not* call up Eliot's poem.

Throughout the book, water is a shorthand sign with multiple meanings. Sometimes, as in Brett's bathing, the need for water is the need to be washed of the moral grime that this novel's flesh is all too heir to. At Pamplona, just after we are told that, like Circe, Brett turns men into swine (144), she says, "I must bathe before dinner." After she has been down cellar with the garlic wreath and the dancing men, she needs a bath (159). After the drunken Pamplona evening during which Jake Barnes pimps for Brett and is knocked out by Cohn, he needs "a deep, hot bath" (193), but when he finds the stone tub, the water will not run. Confession and prayer in the Pamplona church did not make Jake feel much better about his moral condition, and there is no absolution for his acting as a procurer in the Pamplona bar. Montoya will never forgive him for assisting in the corruption of Pedro Romero. Thus it is a fitting sign that Jake finds the deep, stone tub, but the water, when he has most need of it, will not run. At San Sebastian, alone and a little depressed by the Pamplona experience, Jake checks into a hotel and takes a shower (234). After lunch he swims out to the harbor raft, where he finds a young couple talking and laughing. Jake does not tell us to remember that San Sebastian is where Brett took Cohn for their brief fling, but we should make the ironic connection. Jake dives deep in green, dark water, but no amount of water can wash away the week in Pamplona. The sign reminds us of the purification by baptismal water, the holy water that washes the soul clean of original sin. Jake's need is real and deep, but ritual cleansing does not work in modern times.

9 Envoi

Despite its irony and its sadness, we walk away from *The Sun Also Rises* with a good feeling. Maybe we feel that we are not so lost as Jake and his friends. Perhaps we are simply grateful for the guided tour. I suspect, however, it is more than that. No matter how disappointed we are with Brett's behavior or how much we deplore the lack of values, we end up caring about the characters. As Huck Finn told us a long time ago, if you start thinking about them, you end up missing everyone. Jake Barnes was an early explorer of our century's moral condition. That he found it less than grand does not leave us without some hope. Beneath Jake's laconic irony there resides a sense of a better world: because he is dissatisfied with the condition he finds, we know that he has not given up. So too with the reader. So long as we do not approve of the "simple exchange of values," then we know higher standards of behavior exist. Thus, at the moral level, *The Sun Also Rises* is a Horatian satire, gently prodding its readers toward more responsible lives.

I have not discussed everything. I have not expanded the pilgrimage motif, have not said a word about the wonderful landscapes that came out of Cezanne, and have said nothing about style. Readers will recognize that style again without ever understanding it. Knowing is frequently better than understanding. I have provided a rough map of the territory with a few areas more detailed than others. The reader was born with his own compass; from here he can find the way on his own.

Notes

1. Grace Hall Hemingway to Ernest Hemingway, 4 December 1926, Kennedy Library, Boston.

2. Ernest Hemingway to Grace Hemingway, 5 February 1927, *Selected Letters*, ed. Carlos Baker (New York: Charles Scribner's Sons, 1981), 243.

3. "American Bohemians in Paris." *Dateline: Toronto,* ed. William White (New York: Charles Scribner's Sons, 1985), 114.

4. *Dateline Toronto,* 89.

5. R. F. Wilson, *Paris on Parade* (Indianapolis: Bobbs Merrill, 1925), 305–06.

Bibliography

Primary Sources

Across the River and into the Trees. New York: Charles Scribner's Sons, 1950. Paperback. 1970.

By Line: Ernest Hemingway. Edited by William White. New York: Charles Scribner's Sons, 1967. Paperback. New York: Bantam, 1968.

The Dangerous Summer. New York: Charles Scribner's Sons, 1985.

Dateline: Toronto. Edited by William White. New York: Charles Scribner's Sons, 1985.

Death in the Afternoon. New York: Charles Scribner's Sons, 1932. Paperback. 1969.

Eighty-Eight Poems. Edited by Nicholas Gerogiannis. New York: Harcourt Brace, 1979.

A Farewell to Arms. New York: Charles Scribner's Sons, 1929. Paperback. 1962.

The Fifth Column. New York: Charles Scribner's Sons, 1940.

The Fifth Column and the First Forty-Nine Stories. New York: Charles Scribner's Sons, 1938.

For Whom the Bell Tolls. New York: Charles Scribner's Sons, 1940. Paperback. 1960.

The Garden of Eden. New York: Charles Scribner's Sons, 1986.

Green Hills of Africa. New York: Charles Scribner's Sons, 1935. Paperback. 1962.

To Have and Have Not. New York: Charles Scribner's Sons, 1937. Paperback. 1962.

in our time. Paris: Three Mountains Press, 1924.

In Our Time. New York: Boni & Liveright, 1925.

Islands in the Stream. New York: Charles Scribner's Sons, 1970. Paperback. New York: Bantam, 1972.

A Moveable Feast. New York: Charles Scribner's Sons, 1964. Paperback. New York: Bantam, 1965.

The Nick Adams Stories. Edited by Philip Young. New York: Charles Scribner's Sons, 1972.

The Old Man and the Sea. New York: Charles Scribner's Sons, 1952. Paperback. 1965.

Selected Letters 1917–1961. Edited by Carlos Baker. New York: Charles Scribner's Sons, 1981.

The Short Stories of Ernest Hemingway. New York: Charles Scribner's Sons, 1938.

The Sun Also Rises. New York: Charles Scribner's Sons, 1926. Paperback, 1960.

The Sun Also Rises. Manuscript in the J. F. Kennedy Library, Boston, Mass.

Three Stories and Ten Poems. Paris: Contact Publishing Company, 1923.

The Torrents of Spring. New York: Charles Scribner's Sons, 1926. Paperback. 1972.

Secondary Sources

Books

Baker, Carlos. *Hemingway: The Writer as Artist*. Princeton: Princeton University Press, 1952, 1972. Still the best comprehensive view of the total canon.

Baker, Carlos. *Ernest Hemingway, A Life Story*. New York: Scribners, 1969. The standard biography and the most reliable source for who, what, where, when.

Brenner, Gerry. *Concealments in Hemingway's Works*. Ohio State University Press, 1983. Generic and psychoanalytic approaches.

Donaldson, Scott. *By Force of Will*. New York: Viking, 1977. Excellent thematically organized analysis of life and works.

Fitzgerald/Hemingway Annual. Edited by Mathew Bruccoli and C. E. Clark. Washington, D. C.: Microcards Editions. Uneven but wide-ranging collection of articles, biographical studies, memoirs.

Grebstein, Sheldon. *Hemingway's Craft*. Carbondale: Southern Illinois University Press, 1973. Fine study of structure, style, dialogue.

Griffin, Peter. *Along With Youth*. New York: Oxford University Press, 1985. Imaginative but erratic biography; assumes fiction is reality.

The Hemingway Review. Special *SAR* Issue 6 (Fall 1986).

Hemingway, Gregory. *Papa.* New York: Houghton Mifflin, 1976. Freudian and oedipal version of dad by son who was seldom around him.

Hemingway, Leicester. *My Brother, Ernest Hemingway.* New York: World Publishing Co., 1962. Interesting letters quoted. Sibling rivalry. Leicester did not know him well. Good on the home life.

Hemingway, Mary Welsh. *How It Was.* New York: Knopf, 1976. Fourth wife's biography; the difficulties of living with Ernest in his dotage. Good on 1946–61.

Hoffman, Frederick J. *The 20's.* New York: The Free Press, 1954, 1962. Wonderful historical and literary background; treatment as a war novel; chronology of period.

Kert, Bernice. *The Hemingway Women.* New York: Norton, 1983. Excellent study of Hemingway's wives and other loves. Gelhorn material rare.

Loeb, Harold. *The Way It Was.* New York: Criterion Books, 1959. Cohn prototype tells his side of the story.

Meyers, Jeffrey. *Hemingway.* New York: Harper Row, 1985. Full-scale biography. Good on post-1940 period. Good also on literary connections and minor characters.

Reynolds, Michael. *The Young Hemingway.* New York: Basil Blackwell, 1986. Focuses on development as writer before going to Paris: home influences, family medical history, Teddy Roosevelt, historical context.

Rovit, Earl. *Ernest Hemingway.* New York: Twayne, 1963. Rev. Ed. with Gerry Brenner. 1987. Early and still accurate discussion of "code," narrative relationships, style, with fine chapter on *Sun.*

Sanford, Marcelline Hemingway. *At the Hemingway's.* Boston: Little, Brown, 1962. Older sister's attempt to whitewash the family; some nice bits on home life.

Saranson, Bertram D. *Hemingway and the Sun Set.* Washington, D.C.: Microcard Editions, 1972. Biographical: interviews with all prototypes; views of minor players.

Stephens, Robert O. *Hemingway's Nonfiction.* Chapel Hill: University of North Carolina Press, 1968. Useful analysis of nonfiction and the fictional connections.

Svoboda, Frederic J. *Hemingway and The Sun Also Rises.* Lawrence: University of Kansas Press, 1983. Interesting study of manuscript and changes. Generous quotations from original manuscript.

Wagner, Linda W. *Six Decades of Criticism.* East Lansing: Michigan State University Press, 1974, 1987. Strong collection of essays.

Waldhorn, Arthur. *A Reader's Guide to Ernest Hemingway.* New York: Farrar, Straus, 1972. Quick and reliable reference source for who, what, where, when in fiction.

Young, Philip. *Ernest Hemingway, A Reconsideration*. New York: Harcourt, Brace, 1952, 1966. Excellent on psychological and literary connections: the hero and the code; the wounded man; Huck Finn.

Articles

Donaldson, Scott. " 'Irony and Pity'—Anatole France Got It Up." In *Fitzgerald/Hemingway Annual*. Detroit: Gale Research Company, 1978.

Hook, Andrew. "Art and Life in *The Sun Also Rises*." In *Ernest Hemingway: New Critical Essays*. Edited by A. Robert Lee. New York: Barnes and Noble, 1983.

Klug, M. A. "The Horns of Manichaeus: The Conflict of Art and Experience in *The Great Gatsby* and *The Sun Also Rises*." *Essays in Literature* 12 (1985): 111–23.

Kobler, Jasper. "Confused Chronology in *The Sun Also Rises*." *Modern Fiction Studies* 13 (Winter 1967/68):517–20.

Lauter, Paul. "Plato's Stepchildren, Gatsby and Cohn." *Modern Fiction Studies* 9 (Winter 1963/64):338–46.

Moore, Geoffrey. "*The Sun Also Rises*: Notes toward an Extreme Fiction." *Review of English Literature* 4 (October 1963):31–46.

Murphy, George D. "Hemingway's *Waste Land*: The Controlling Water Symbolism of *The Sun Also Rises*." *Hemingway Notes* 1 (Spring 1971):20–26.

Reynolds, Michael. "False Dawn: A Preliminary Analysis of *The Sun Also Rises* Manuscript." In *Hemingway: A Revaluation*. Edited by Donald R. Noble. New York: Whitston Publishing Company, 1983.

Ross, Morton. "Bill Gorton the Preacher in *The Sun Also Rises*." *Modern Fiction Studies* 18 (Winter 1972/73):517–27.

Rouch, John. "Jake Barnes as Narrator." *Modern Fiction Studies* 11 (Winter 1965/66):361–70.

Spilka, Mark. "The Love of Death in *The Sun Also Rises*." In *Hemingway and His Critics*. Edited by Carlos Baker. New York: Hill and Wang, 1961.

Sprague, Claire. "*The Sun Also Rises*: 'Its Clear Financial Basis.' " *American Quarterly* 21 (Summer 1969):259–66.

Stoneback. H. R. "With Hemingway and Faulkner on the Road to Roncevaux." in *Hemingway: A Revaluation*. Edited by Donald R. Noble. New York: Whitston Publishing Company, 1983.

Vanderbilt, Kermit. "*The Sun Also Rises*: Time Uncertain." *Twentieth Century Literature* 15 (October 1969):153–54.

Wagner, Linda. "*The Sun Also Rises*: One Debt to Imagism." *Journal of Narrative Technique* 2 (May 1972):88–98.

Bibliography and Reference

Brasch, James and Joseph Sigman. *Hemingway's Library.* New York: Garland, 1981. Over 7000 books which were in Hemingway's Key West library or with him in Cuba 1940–59.

Hanneman, Audre. *Ernest Hemingway: A Comprehensive Bibliography.* Princeton: Princeton University Press, 1967. Both primary and secondary; an excellent bibliography that includes most newspaper and periodical articles on Hemingway.

———. *Supplement to Ernest Hemingway.* Princeton: Princeton University Press, 1975.

Reynolds, Michael S. *Hemingway's Reading: 1910–1940.* Princeton: Princeton University Press, 1981. Over 2000 items read or owned by Hemingway, including Key West. Overlaps with Brasch and Sigman.

Stephens, Robert O. *Ernest Hemingway, the Critical Reception.* New York: Burt Franklin, 1977. Generous selections from first and follow-up reviews of all the works.

Index

Index

About the Author

Michael Reynolds, a professor of English at North Carolina State University, has published four books and numerous articles, almost all of which have focused on Ernest Hemingway. His books include: *Hemingway's First War* (1976), a study of the making of *A Farewell to Arms; Hemingway's Reading: 1910–1940* (1981), an inventory of what Hemingway read and when he read it; an edited collection, *Critical Essays on Hemingway's "In Our Time"* (1983); and *The Young Hemingway* (1986), a literary biography of the early years which was a finalist in the American Book Awards and was nominated for the Pulitzer Prize in biography. Professor Reynolds is now at work on the second volume of the literary biography covering Hemingway's Paris years.